FURTWÄNGLER AND AMERICA

CONCERT IN BERLIN, 1949

by Rudolf Kessle

Furtwängler and America

by DANIEL GILLIS

Manyland Books, Inc. • New York

MANYLAND BOOKS, INC.
84-39 90th Street
Woodhaven, N. Y. 11421

Library of Congress Catalogue Card No. 75-125028

SBN 87141-031-1

MANUFACTURED IN THE UNITED STATES OF AMERICA

PREFACE

I wish to express my gratitude briefly to several friends who have been helpful to me in the preparation of this book: Ernö Balogh, Suzanne Bloch, Karla Hoecker, Margaret Kolmar, Louis P. Lochner, Moshe Menuhin, J. Vernon Patrick, Jr., and Annalise Wiener. I am especially grateful to Frau Elisabeth Furtwängler for having kindly opened to me the files of her husband's correspondence. Elsewhere, in *Furtwängler Recalled*, an assessment of the conductor's art has been made by many musicians and critics. The present work is largely political—inevitably, because Furtwängler's life was so deeply scarred by politics.

DANIEL GILLIS

Haverford, Penna.
February 1970.

I

LATE IN 1967, in his notes for the Seraphim recording of
Furtwängler's *Fidelio,* Karl Schumann wrote that

">. . . For forty years the name of Wilhelm Furtwängler
has been looked upon as an authority in the cultivation
of good taste in questions of music, as a guarantee for
an esoteric interpretation and as a yardstick by which
the greatness of a conductor is measured. Furtwängler has
moulded the picture of Beethoven and Brahms of two
generations. His personality, which has been elevated
from the level of the generally accepted conception of a
conductor to that of a myth, has become nothing short
of an ideal, not restricted to the confines of Germany,
and this reputation has in no way been altered through
his death. Whoever conducts Beethoven, Brahms, Wagner and Bruckner today finds himself, consciously or
unconsciously, competing against the overpowering shad-
ow of Furtwängler."

This accurate appraisal of Wilhelm Furtwängler's continuing role in German and European musical life does not, as
yet, apply to the United States. Most Furtwängler recordings are now available here; the reputation of the artist is
secure among record collectors, and in fact is growing. But

among the larger contemporary public, especially younger people, the name is both unpronounceable and of no particular significance. The task of this study will be to trace how this situation has arisen, how pressures were exerted several times in order to exclude Furtwängler from America. This country has a history of mistreating artists—at one time or another Gustav Mahler, Fritz Kreisler, Karl Muck, Otto Klemperer and Josef Krips have been humiliated and rejected here—but in none of these cases was such a heavy price exacted: the ostracism of a man recognized by Europe and its finest musicians as the greatest conductor of the century.

In order to understand how this happened, one must begin in Carnegie Hall in New York City, on January 3, 1925, when Wilhelm Furtwängler faced his first American audience. In an era of many famous Central European conductors—Walter, Klemperer, Busch, Weingartner, Muck, Krauss, Kleiber and others were all active—he came acknowledged as the logical heir to the great Arthur Nikisch as Permanent Conductor of the Berlin Philharmonic and Leipzig Gewandhaus Orchestras. He was thirty-nine years old. His career had been one of steady success, carved out on purely artistic grounds amid capable rivals and before gifted audiences; and now he had come to New York to conquer America. His program that evening was the Haydn *D Major 'Cello Concerto* with Pablo Casals as soloist, *Don Juan* of Strauss, and the Brahms *First Symphony*. He stunned his audience. The next day, Olin Downes, perhaps the most powerful of New York music critics, wrote in the *Times*:

> ". . . There was a communicative fire in everything that he did, flame that burned clear and bright within him. But it was a selfless spirit that showed in the face of the man and inspired the players. Not all

the performances were to be accepted without reservation, but they invariably revealed the stature of a true musician, and the performance of the Brahms C Minor Symphony was perhaps the most thrilling in the writer's experience. . . . The audience found last night that nothing was more stirring than simply Brahms's C Minor Symphony. There was enough in that to absorb and stir to the depths the conductor and the listeners. Yet a performance more carefully thought out, more scrupulously proportioned, delivered with deeper devotion to letter as well as meaning would be hard to imagine. . . . It was high time that such an interpretation should take place here. Regardless of what the sum of Mr. Furtwängler's efforts as guest conductor of the Philharmonic may prove to be, he has accomplished one thing which will be gratefully remembered and looked back to as an inspiration to those who were present. . . . This performance swept everything before it by reason of its vitality, the irresistible and unbroken current of its rhythms, and the spirit of greatness and heroism that informed every measure. It was not astonishing that the audience cheered as well as applauded as the last chord sounded."

Furtwängler gave several other concerts in January 1925, playing some of the works on which he had built his career —the Schumann *Fourth,* the Tchaikovsky *Fifth,* Weber's *Freischütz Overture*—but also introducing Stravinsky's *Sacre du Printemps* to the Philharmonic. Downes challenged some of the "personal leanings" Furtwängler had revealed in his performances, but the public filled the hall to standing room and gave him eight or nine curtain calls after each concert. The final concert on January 30—the Haydn *Surprise Symphony,* Strauss's *Death and Transfiguration,* and the Beethoven *Fifth*—was fully as triumphant as the first. The *Times* reported the next day:

"Fifteen minutes' cheering on the public's part finished a personal tribute to Wilhelm Furtwängler at last night's special Philharmonic concert at Carnegie Hall in honor of the guest conductor who sails aboard the *Minnetonka* today for Germany. From the veteran orchestra's one hundred players, who joined in the applause, he had received a great silver loving cup at the preceding morning rehearsals, while after the concert Furtwängler was their guest at a supper in the musicians' assembly room in Carnegie Hall. 'I hope to come back,' the conductor said in his speech of thanks at the morning presentation, 'and I hope you will all be here next season.' "

The article assessed the Haydn and Strauss performances, then referred to Furtwängler's innovation in restraining applause between movements of a symphony.

"Hissing is a rarity in New York. It was heard as a quick, popular reinforcement of the conductor's forbidding hand when some in the house started applause between movements of the closing symphony last night. . . . Thrice deferred, the hearers' enthusiasm found vent in fifteen minutes of "Bravos!"

Chairman Clarence H. Mackay of the Philharmonic Board and the conductor Willem Mengelberg, here to complete the orchestra's season, were in the audience, whose quality represented old-time New York subscribers to both the Philharmonic Society and the Boston Symphony. A nonsubscription host of musicians and musical enthusiasts included at least one entire musical staff of a Broadway motion picture house, representatives of the theatre and art world, society and letters, who shouted 'Come back next year!' "

Furtwängler had good reason to believe he had conquered New York. He had not pleased the critics as much as he had pleased his audiences, but he hated critics and thought he could ignore them. Coming from a European tradition of state subsidies for orchestral organizations, he was totally unaware of the tremendous importance and power of private

12

patrons and patronesses in American orchestral circles. He had never been expected to be especially polite to officials of state, in fact he had refused to salute the Kaiser and later the leaders of the Weimar Republic before his concerts in Berlin because he thought this undignified; and now he did not feel the necessity to show any particular attention to the Chairman and members of the Philharmonic Board, or to the patrons and patronesses of the Philharmonic Society. Consequently he had unwittingly offended many; he had often been invited to receptions in his honor by the most exclusive circles in New York, and he had spent his evenings at them discussing musical interpretation with his musicians. The ladies of the Philharmonic Society felt slighted. And even at the end of this highly successful visit, no public honors were forthcoming from Clarence H. Mackay and his Board; the support came from the Orchestra itself and its audience.

There was perhaps another reason for this. Unknown to Furtwängler, Mackay had been trying for years to bring Arturo Toscanini, then Director of La Scala, to conduct the Philharmonic. He had heard the Italian conductor at the Metropolitan Opera in the early part of the century, and again during Toscanini's American visit with the Scala orchestra in 1921; he hoped now to secure his services as symphonic conductor. Negotiations had been going on while Furtwängler was in New York, and in June 1925, it was announced that Toscanini would come as a Guest Conductor during the following season. The *Times* devoted nearly half a page to an article by F. L. Minnegerode entitled "Milan Will Lend Us Maestro Toscanini" on June 14; and shortly before Toscanini's first appearance, Downes wrote another lengthy feature article. The original announcement of Furtwängler's appointment had been given two paragraphs in the *Times* on July 30, 1924.

It is worth examining this feature article by Downes

because it throws considerable light on his subsequent treatment of Furtwängler. Like Mackay, Downes had been a devoted admirer of Toscanini during his tenure at the Metropolitan; though he had rarely heard Toscanini as a symphonic conductor, Downes had no hesitation in proclaiming:

> "If ever there was a man who justified the theory of aristocracy built upon the fundamental conception that men are not born free and equal, that some are immeasurably superior to others, and that their superiority is justification for their control of others' acts and destinies, that man is Arturo Toscanini. Outside of his art we need not question or discuss him, nor make a matter for academic argument the question of the attitude of the individual toward his fellows. In that sphere, which is the freest and highest playground for the human spirit, he stands as a hero and a master; one who has never yielded an inch to self-interest or expediency; who is completely and unmistakably contemptuous of such matters as public praise or financial gain, and who has kept the flame of his art through every fact of existence clear and bright and intense. It is with something more than the curiosity that awaits the appearance of a famous guest conductor that the Philharmonic audiences will gather to meet Mr. Toscanini."

Such intense admiration for Toscanini had never been lavished on Furtwängler or any other conductor; clearly Downes was already quite committed to his idol. Elsewhere in the same article he had expressed his racist preference for the Italian mind, even when it was interpreting alien music:

> "In listening to operatic and orchestral interpretations of Toscanini it has often seemed that after all the statement holds true of the quality of the Italian mind, the racial mind that has the finest facture of any in the world; the genius which, at its height, combines marvelously the qualities of analysis and perception, the

14

objectivity of form, and the consuming fire of creative passion."

This preference lay at the root of Downes's increasingly critical approach to Furtwängler's "Germanic" conducting. When he reviewed Furtwängler's first concert of the second season, he duly noted the impressive demonstration of welcome when the conductor stepped on the stage. He also noted the "Made in Germany" program—Beethoven's *Egmont Overture*, Mozart's *Eine Kleine Nachtmusik*, Brahms's *Fourth Symphony*, and Wagner's *Meistersinger Prelude*. The review had some good things to say; but Downes also spoke of Furtwängler's "deviation from traditional usage," his "occasional roughness and weight," adding that "his enthusiasm and his energy ran away with him, so that the tone was now and again rough and noisy" in the Wagner work. But more important than these criticisms was Downes's firm challenge to Furtwängler's insistence on silence between movements of the Mozart and Beethoven pieces.

"The conductor signalled for no applause after each of the movements. This practice has been referred to on several occasions in these columns, with the remark that it often detracts from the effect of the music and the audience's enjoyment of it. Certainly it is hard to believe that Mozart would have advised any such treatment of four movements written in the lighter vein, for no purpose more profound than that of pleasure and entertainment. Why an audience should sit through such a performance as seriously and silently as if it were listening to Bach's B Minor Mass is a question that will obtrude itself, even on the auspicious occasion of Mr. Furtwängler's opening American concert of the year 1926...."

The irritation of Downes that the public was siding with Furtwängler in spite of his own frequent remarks in favor

15

of spontaneous applause, is clear enough here; but at the close of his review he had to admit that

> ". . . There was long applause, certain groups cheering and remaining demonstrative until the conductor refused longer to come upon the stage. Mr. Furtwängler had reason to feel gratified with his reception."

His reviews became less and less favorable. Furtwängler became more and more angry with them and suggested that the *Times* send a more musical crtic to his concerts. Downes was then irreconcilable. By now he had lost the dispute over applause; and his original pro-Toscanini bias now became more clearly anti-Furtwängler. In January, Toscanini had led his first series of concerts amid all the heraldry Downes and the Philharmonic publicity office could give him; yet he left without a gift from the orchestra and without the wildly enthusiastic farewell demonstration Furtwängler had enjoyed a year earlier. And in February, at the end of Furtwängler's second visit, the Philharmonic Board felt it necessary to deny widespread rumors that Furtwängler would soon be named Permanent Conductor of the Philharmonic.

Rumors of a different kind preceded Furtwängler's arrival for his third New York season. On January 20, 1927, the *Times* reported

> ". . . Following a rumor that the Philharmonic and the New York Symphony Orchestra might amalgamate came another yesterday that negotiations had fallen in. It earlier appeared that on the Philharmonic side those favoring a single orchestra desired to divide the next season between Willem Mengelberg, the Dutch conductor, and Toscanini."

Toscanini had been unable to conduct the first two weeks of his engagement, because of a grippe infection resulting from overwork. A week later the *Times* of January 26 reported that

> "The veil of mystery that for three weeks has surrounded Mr. Toscanini's failure to conduct the Philharmonic Orchestra, for which he had accepted a month's contract and had made the voyage to America, was broken at last at yesterday morning's rehearsal of the orchestra in Carnegie Hall. Contrary to many reports, it was made known that the conductor would appear publicly before sailing back to Italy.
>
> Mr. Toscanini, it was announced later in the day, had agreed to undertake three concerts here and one in Philadelphia. These constituted all that would remain of his schedule before Mr. Furtwängler's return.
>
> As his appearances were so limited, Toscanini decided a Beethoven festival would be 'interesting and timely.' This he would open with two Beethoven symphonies at the Metropolitan Opera House concert next Tuesday night, the Third or 'Eroica,' and the Fifth.
>
> The Ninth Symphony will follow at both the Saturday night 'students' concert' and the concert Sunday afternoon, February 6, in Carnegie Hall. It will be preceded by the First Symphony, and the singers for the choral Ninth will be those already prepared by the Schola Cantorum.
>
> . . . As lately as yesterday morning, published reports had Mr. Toscanini quitting the United States for a year of rest. It was hinted that memorizing music, which he invariably leads without a score, had become too taxing for him. A denial of that was promptly issued by Dr. Hubert Howe, personal physician to the Philharmonic Chairman, Clarence H. Mackay.
>
> Mr. Mackay is understood to have underwritten half of the cost, both last season and again this year, of bringing Toscanini to America. He prevailed on the conductor, who had missed three weeks of concerts while convalescent from grip at the Hotel Astor, to end all further doubt and delay by publicly redeeming the final weeks of his engagement as announced."

Thus Toscanini, now quite recovered, though his physician had reportedly advised a long rest, agreed to conduct two Beethoven programs in honor of the hundredth anniversary of the composer's death. The second was to feature the *Ninth*, with singers "already prepared by the Schola Cantorum." The singers had indeed been prepared for the *Ninth*—but it was to have been Furtwängler's *Ninth*. Mackay invited RCA to broadcast Toscanini's *Ninth* on WJZ with the words:

> "My fellow executives of the Philharmonic Society and I believe that these concerts are of such importance that they should be made available to as great a public as possible, and in presenting them to the great 'invisible' audience we are following out the rapidly expanding educational policy of the Society."

This "rapidly expanding educational policy" of the Philharmonic was not to include Furtwängler.

He arrived on the same day as the statement by Mackay was made known, and in reply to queries whether he would succeed Walter Damrosch as head of the New York Symphony, he said that he knew nothing of such a proposal and that he was very well satisfied with his present position. The Toscanini *Ninth* was accompanied by a feature article, half a page in length, written by Downes, entitled "Toscanini's Beethoven." At the conclusion of the concert on February 6, where a more enthusiastic audience than he had ever experienced in Carnegie Hall loudly expressed its gratitude for his return in the face of illness, Toscanini was given a laurel wreath with two hundred American Beauty roses and an inscription from the Chairman and Board of Directors of the Philharmonic Society. For the second time he left without recognition from the Orchestra itself.

Furtwängler, who was to have conducted the *Ninth* at

his final concert, was shocked at the arbitrary decision by the Philharmonic Board to transfer this program to Toscanini. He told a friend in New York, Albrecht Pagenstecher —as Pagenstecher recalled the incident many years later— that he had learned that Toscanini's illness had been feigned and that Toscanini had threatened to cancel all his commitments and return to Italy unless he was allowed to conduct the *Ninth* in place of Furtwängler. Now Furtwängler realized that he had no friends on the Board. Mackay was fully prepared to grant Toscanini his wish, in order that he resume conducting: the annual guarantee, reportedly fifty thousand dollars, would have to be paid even if he did not lead the Orchestra again. Weighed against this, Furtwängler's pride hardly mattered.

On March 4, the Philharmonic office announced

"... with regret that it has been found impossible on the part of both the Society and Mr. Furtwängler to arrange satisfactory dates for the latter's visit to America next season.

Mr. Furtwängler, as conductor of the most important musical organizations in Europe, has been compelled to commit himself to certain obligations which unfortunately cannot be coördinated with the time which the Philharmonic has available.

Mr. Mackay, however, takes pleasure in announcing that the Society has an arrangement with Mr. Furtwängler whereby he will be available for the Philharmonic Society for the three seasons, beginning with the concert season of 1928-29. ..."

The public was amazed at this statement, and there was wide speculation that the Philharmonic was not telling the truth. In fact, Furtwängler had no prior obligations conflicting with a visit to the Philharmonic the next year. Several angry letters appeared in the *Times:*

"Is there a conspiracy against Wilhelm Furtwängler, or is it the usual psychological phenomenon of the New York public bringing about the fall of this god? When this eminent conductor first appeared, the critics told us that he electrified the orchestra. . . . Furtwängler is no less capable, no less inspired than he was two years ago. . . . Were he to conduct Tchaikovsky's Fourth and Sixth frequently enough, not even the critics could shake him down from his pedestal. He does not cater. He is an artist and therefore probably a very poor politician. . . . Unfortunately, public opinion is formed by critics, and their coolness toward Furtwängler must be politics. This is of course a presumption. Why all of a sudden, when Toscanini conducts, forget everyone, and knock Furtwängler especially? It isn't fair play and it is with profound regret that I look upon the absence of this sincere artist who consistently refuses to prostitute his art for applause and the favor of critics."

Another letter blamed the Philharmonic Board:

"The fact that Mr. Furtwängler is not returning next season has little or nothing to do with his ability or his obvious popularity with his audiences, and with the all too little considered minority—the Philharmonic Orchestra. Why, then, are we about to lose the services of this man who is surely one of the world's greatest conductors and is appreciated as such in every musical community but this? . . . Among the (Philharmonic) directors, whom we must admire for their sacrifice of time and money to art, there are not those in any way qualified to pass judgment on the musical qualities of a great composer, a great conductor, or a great soloist. Their judgment of artists is largely influenced by the latter's personality and capability of producing the sensational. Art is the outcome of sincerity, understanding and repose. Sensationalism is an artificial hypodermic. . . . Should not, therefore, the vote of large competent bodies such as orchestras and the expressed taste of the public, measured in applause and box-office receipts, be

considered in determining whether a conductor be
engaged or not?"

Olin Downes felt the necessity to defend at length his
hostile reviews of Furtwängler's concerts against what he
termed "extreme opinions" of those who had written the
Times. In a feature article, "Furtwängler's Conductorship,"
on March 27, he marshalled many "facts" to support his
views, never admitting that musical criticism could be based
on anything else.

"The *Times* publishes today letters from supporters of
Wilhelm Furtwängler, who protest against the conclusion of his engagement as conductor of the Philharmonic Orchestra. The grounds taken for these protests
are substantially those raised in other letters published
in these columns of late weeks, since the announcement
of Mr. Furtwängler's departure. The assertion is made,
and apparently believed by certain correspondents, that
the termination of Mr. Furtwängler's engagement is due
to a lack of appreciation of his work and even hostility
toward him on the part of the critics. It is deduced from
these premises that the critics have influenced an un-
thinking public to stay away from Mr. Furtwängler's
concerts and have prejudiced the management of the
Philharmonic so that it has failed to reengage him. To
these general observations is added the insinuation, to
be noted in another column, that the men or the man
principally responsible for the politics of the Philharmonic are not sufficiently informed on matters pertain-
ing to the musical art to know what conductor it is
best for them to engage, or whose advice to take in
determining so important a question.
   The facts are otherwise than the letters of Mr. Furtwängler's adherents would indicate. A consensus of critical opinion, coming from different quarters, without
the slightest prejudice or collusion, has rated Mr. Furtwängler's performances less highly than those of either
of his colleagues, Messrs. Mengelberg and Toscanini of

21

the Philharmonic, this season. It has not been the design or the pleasure of the reviewers concerned to give expressions to these estimates. With one of them, at least, it has been a matter of private regret and disappointment that a conductor who promised as greatly as Mr. Furtwängler when first he arrived in New York should fall so far below his early standards. . . . Mr. Furtwängler has not maintained during the season anything like the technical and artistic level of his opening and historic performance of Brahms's *First Symphony* with the Philharmonic Orchestra. This is not opinion but fact. There are and there have been many minor divergencies of opinion concerning this or that Furtwängler performance.

There have been paragraphs and articles of praise as well as blame for him, and often a point has been stretched to give encouragement where needed. Contrary to having been treated with prejudice by the press of this city, Mr. Furtwängler has been treated with distinguished consideration, but frequently his performances have been characterized by sentimentality, a tension and vacillation unfavorable to their effect and to the nature of reviews that inevitably followed. Reviewers are not to be blamed if they are obliged to record things in a manner other than the Polyanna style that some people uphold as the rightful standard of musical criticism.

But there is another element in this situation more important, more determinate by far, and far less subject to influences of written criticism than many believe. We refer to the verdict of the public. It is a fact that may be ascertained by the curious that the public, which originally greeted Mr. Furtwängler with warm and spontaneous acclaim, has given its silent verdict upon his performances by patronizing them in lesser degree than it patronized the performances of his fellow-conductors. This is a matter which must and should count with a great orchestral organization. . . .

Another matter which touches directly upon the public interest is the apparent limitation of Mr. Furtwängler's repertory. Like many other German conductors lacking wide experience outside their own country, his repertory has been limited, particularly in his first two seasons, and when he ventured outside the stock German repertory it was not always with happy results. German conductors as a class, when they come to America, have to outgrow certain nationalistic musical leanings. It is often astonishing and sometimes unwelcome to them to discover that American audiences are accustomed to a broad and catholic repertory; that American standards of performance are considerably higher—not lower, but higher than those which obtain today in Europe; and, finally, that by virtue of sheer wealth, if nothing else, there come to American cities such as New York many great conductors of various nationalities whom the public estimates regardless of their foreign reputation and entirely upon the merits of their performances.

It is hardly to be gainsaid by unprejudiced individuals that in point of variety of programs and also sympathetic insight into music of different periods, nationalities and schools, Mr. Furtwängler's nearest competitors have surpassed him. It is also a fact that the technical standards of the Philharmonic under Messrs. Mengelberg and Toscanini have been for virtuoso finish and beauty of tone superior to those of Mr. Furtwängler. These are hard things to say, but it seems that the time has come when a few plain words are desirable in reply to unfounded charges and extreme opinions.

One more observation is due to the wise and admirable actions of Mr. Mackay and his associates in their development to its present high level of artistic accomplishment of the Philharmonic Orchestra, an orchestra which is now one of the very best in the country. For years they had made efforts to bring Mr. Toscanini to this city as head of the Philharmonic. At last they succeeded. Their efforts were completely justified by the results. Mr. Toscanini was recognized as one of the greatest if not the greatest conductor who has led either the Philharmonic or any other American orchestra in recent years. Mr. Toscanini has gained by virtue of his genius

23

and nothing else, the admiration and support of reviewers and audiences wherever and whenever he appeared.
He has put a fine edge on the technical accomplishment
of an orchestra heavily indebted for its technical standards to the faithful labors of Willem Mengelberg. Mr.
Mengelberg, in turn, during his half of the Philharmonic
season which has just ended, gave more interesting programs and more brilliant performances than he had
achieved in his two preceding engagements. If, as many
have claimed, the sensational successes of Toscanini af-
fected both Mengelberg and Furtwängler in their spirits
and accomplishments, the response of Mr. Mengelberg
was extremely impressive and gave further evidence of
his great inherent qualities as a musician and conductor.
Under these circumstances it does not appear to the
present commentator, and it is not the majority opinion,
that the direction of the Philharmonic has shown anything less than sound sense and high artistic policy in
re-engaging Messrs. Mengelberg and Toscanini for next
year—it having been stated that Mr. Furtwängler could
not come to America at that time—and in having pre-
vailed upon Mr. Toscanini to stay, if his health permits,
from the time Mr. Mengelberg leaves to the end of the
1927-28 Philharmonic season."

Some readers of the *Times* sharply disagreed. One correspondent took exception to the charge that Furtwängler
was limited in his repertory:

". . . Mr. Downes must surely remember the mellifluous
words and the gallant phrases he used to denote the
grandiloquence of Furtwängler's presentation of Tchaikovsky's *Fifth Symphony*. . . . Mr. Deems Taylor has
rated Furtwängler as second only to Karl Muck, and
Mr. W. J. Henderson, only last year, called the performance of Dvorak's *"New World" Symphony* the
greatest he had ever heard—and he heard the immortal
Nikisch introduce it! And what have become of the
eulogies showered on Herr Furtwängler for his *"Pathétique" Symphony*, for his Brahms *Fourth Symphony*,

for the exquisite accompaniment to the Schumann piano concerto? Alas, they, too, melted away. . . ."

It was hardly correct to charge Furtwängler with "nationalistic musical leanings" when he had performed works by Stravinsky, Ravel, Prokofiev, Berlioz, Dvorak, Respighi, Sibelius, Miaskovsky, Valentini, Tchaikovsky, Saint-Saëns, Franck, and the American composer Ernest Schelling.[1] Another reader challenged further claims by Downes:

". . . I know leading musicians in New York who feel that Mr. Furtwängler has not fallen below his early standards, but maintained the highest ideals and interpretations.

You made the point that public patronage must be considered. 'A symphonic orchestra,' you wrote, 'is making propaganda not for a conductor, or a nationality, or anything but music. If one conductor attracts smaller audiences than another, the public will benefit the less by the orchestra's ministrations.' Aren't you, in saying this, establishing a standard of quantity rather than of quality? If Mr. Babe Ruth were to lead the Philharmonic he would probably draw larger audiences than Messrs. Furtwängler, Mengelberg and Toscanini put together. Would that mean that the public would therefore benefit, musically, more by Mr. Ruth's conducting?

In conclusion, I believe that there is some justice in your criticism of Mr. Furtwängler's repertory. But didn't you commit an unconscious error of fact when you described Mr. Furtwängler with the phrase, 'like many other German conductors lacking wide experience outside their own country?' You surely know that he has conducted not only in the cities of Breslau, Zürich, Munich, Strasbourg, Lübeck, Mannheim, Berlin, Leipzig and Vienna, but also in various cities of England, Swe-

---

[1] See John Erskine, *The Philharmonic-Symphony Society of New York. Its First Hundred Years* (New York, The Macmillan Company, 1943), pp. 90-101.

den, Denmark, Switzerland, and elsewhere. That isn't exactly a narrow foreign experience."[2]

And B. H. Haggin, writing in the condescending style he was later to cultivate in treating Furtwängler, provided an original view of Furtwängler's alleged "deterioration," and then some facts about actual events in his final season:

> "One can explain the quality of Furtwängler's first performances as the excessive response of the Philharmonic musicians (exceeding the demands actually made upon them) to a conductor at once new and competent. Then the quality of his most recent performances becomes the measure of his own limited, if genuine, competence. (At that, the audience also responded excessively and for the same reasons. If it found Furtwängler's performance of Brahms's C Minor extraordinary, it was in part because it had not listened to Mengelberg with as much attention and expectancy. There is significance in the fact that the one man who began and ended by dissenting from the prevailing opinion was Ernest Newman, who was already familiar with his work from European hearings.)
>
> But the drop in quality is not such as one might suppose from your article, nor such as would affect the size of the audience. In tonal quality the best of Furtwängler's performances have been superior to many of Mengelberg's. On the other hand, Furtwängler does not, as Mengelberg does, seem able to grasp and project the structure of a work as an integrated whole, and his performances therefore lack Mengelberg's grip and miss

---

[2] By 1927 Furtwängler had also conducted in Italy and Hungary. His experience in symphonic conducting outside his homeland surpassed, in fact, that of Toscanini, whose full-time symphonic career began in New York with his first visit in 1926. An artist raised in a nation with an operatic, not a symphonic, tradition, Toscanini had previously given his primary allegiance to opera. Mengelberg noted with wry amusement in 1930 that Toscanini did not know symphonic repertoire. A somewhat similar phenomenon occurs at present, with the arrival of young star conductors, who are still learning repertoire, at the peak of their profession.

consummation; but they just miss it and come near enough to be acceptable by the Philharmonic audience, if one may judge by the absurd claims of your correspondents.

For the public has given no such verdict as you speak of. The facts seem to be that there is an audience of definite size that comes to Philharmonic concerts on ordinary occasions; that it takes an extraordinary occasion to attract in addition those whom only extraordinary occasions will attract; that Furtwängler, like Mengelberg, no longer attracts these additional people because he is no longer an extraordinary occasion; and that Toscanini, as Mr. Henderson has already suggested, will also cease to attract them when he ceases to be an extraordinary occasion.

If, then, the Philharmonic management has been influenced by the size of Furtwängler's audiences, this is only additional evidence that it is open to insinuations concerning its competence."

It seems unlikely that Downes was unaware that he, as one of New York's leading critics, had helped stimulate an atmosphere wherein creative work was difficult for Furtwängler—and this for personal reasons.[3] It seems equally unlikely that he was unaware of the background of Toscanini's illness, of the obvious favoritism in publicity given to Toscanini by Mackay and his Board, or of the incident of the *Ninth,* when he wrote, "Mr. Toscanini has gained by virtue of his genius and nothing else the support of reviewers and audiences." Was the "majority opinion" really unfavorable to Furtwängler as Downes claimed?[4] His own de-

---

[3] Downes' personal bitterness did not end with Furtwängler's elimination. In 1930, while visiting Suzanne Bloch, he noticed a photograph of Furtwängler on her piano and exclaimed, "Take that swine's picture away from there!"

[4] Joseph Szigeti, who had been soloist at one of Furtwängler's last concerts in 1927, recounted "the uneasy, strained atmosphere backstage, the demonstrative ovations out front that seemed to protest against a 'fait accompli' . . . and the resigned, forgiving smile of the obviously hurt artist, a

scription of Furtwängler's performance of Brahms's *German Requiem* a few days later suggests that it was not.

'. . . The occasion was impressive. There was long applause and cheers from parts of the auditorium when Mr. Furtwängler appeared upon the stage. The orchestra rose to greet him. It was arranged that there should be an intermission after the third number of the *Requiem*. When this ended applause broke out. Mr. Furtwängler silenced it with a gesture, and this was well, since, although the music was given in a concert hall, there was profound and indeed religious feeling in the interpretation.
. . . This was one of the best performances Mr. Furtwängler has given in New York City, and one of those for which he will be longest and most gratefully remembered by his audiences. . . .
After the concert the audience remained for some minutes in the hall applauding and Mr. Furtwängler was given a wreath in recognition of his services with the Philharmonic. . . ."

On April 4, a *Times* report of the final Furtwängler concert at the Metropolitan Opera House presented a similar scene of public support for Furtwängler:

". . . After Brahms's solemn finale, *Blessed Are the Dead Which Die in the Lord,* an audience that filled the floor and galleries broke its silence to bring out Conductor Furtwängler and the artists, chorus and orchestra for a succession of rising recalls. Even when the stage was cleared and the crowd was dispersing many lingered to applaud. Mr. Furtwängler bowed but did not, as at Carnegie Hall, attempt a speech . . .
Mr. Furtwängler shook hands with the veteran cellist

---

smile that seemed to answer the acclaim with a philosophical 'too late!' . . ."
Cf. *Furtwängler Recalled,* edited by Daniel Gillis (Zürich, Atlantis Verlag and Tuckahoe, New York, John DeGraff, Inc., 1966), p. 140.

Leo Schulz and with the concertmasters and others of the orchestra as he bade the Philharmonic farewell . . ."

And in the *Times* on July 9, 1939, in a less defensive mood than was evident in "Furtwängler's Conductorship," Downes recalled this article and admitted in effect that the unfavorable "majority opinion" and the public's "silent verdict" against Furtwängler were myths.

"When, of the three conductors of a certain Philharmonic-Symphony season, Mengelberg and Toscanini were invited to return, while the re-engagement of Furtwängler was not announced, his partisans wrote furious letters to the newspapers. The critics, it was claimed, were in a cabal against Furtwängler. The Maecenas who handsomely remedied the deficits of the Philharmonic-Symphony season—the late Clarence Mackay—was acting on the bad advice of these critics, and other bigoted persons, in parting with the greatest of the conductors who directed his orchestra.

This partisanship at last occasioned a reply from one of the embattled critics in the form of an article which aroused a tempest in a teapot. The article was protested by the Furtwängler partisans, and warmly commended by the opposing camp. Indignation meetings were held. When Furtwängler made his appearance at a concert attended by the author of the said article there was ferocious applause as he stepped upon the stage, while those seated near glared at the offending writer. . . ."[5]

So it was that Furtwängler left America on April 7, 1927. This was the first time he had been humiliated by the backroom politics of American musical circles, and it was not to be the last. Mackay's statement that an agreement had been made with Furtwängler for a return in 1928 and later seasons

[5] No letters from the "opposing camp" had appeared in the *Times* warmly commending this article.

was merely a face-saving gesture. Mengelberg was removed a few years later, though he had helped forge the Philharmonic and the New York Symphony into a unified instrument. Between 1927 and 1932, Clemens Krauss, Fritz Reiner, Erich Kleiber, Leopold Stokowski, Sir Thomas Beecham, Ossip Gabrilowitsch, Arthur Honegger, Bernardino Molinari, and Vladimir Golschmann, among others, were invited to lead the Orchestra as Guest Conductors. Furtwängler was not.

II

FURTWÄNGLER returned to musical life in the great cities of Europe, touring alone and with the Berlin Philharmonic, assuming as well the Principal Conductorship of the Vienna Philharmonic, enjoying great acclaim wherever he went. In 1932, he was awarded the Goethe Medal of the German Government in recognition of his services to German music; this honor came as part of the Berlin Philharmonic's fiftieth anniversary celebrations. Furtwängler introduced the young Paul Hindemith's *Philharmonic Concerto*, written for the occasion. He delivered an address on the value of the Berlin Philharmonic to Germany and the help it needed to survive in the Depression, and in the course of this address he compared its founding as a necessary part of cultural life to the "Luxushunden" or "luxury pups" that were American orchestras. Though a minor point in an important speech, this was emphasized in the American press and provoked sharp criticism here. Furtwängler was surprised that such a passing remark was so exaggerated, but in the published version of his text he changed the term to "luxury articles" to avoid further offense.

Louis P. Lochner, Chief of The Associated Press Bureau

in Berlin, wrote him that American orchestral groups depended to a large extent on the hard work and faithful contributions of active private groups, and that attempts were being made to enlarge the musical public here by "pop" and stadium concerts in various parts of the country, intended for the common man in whatever station in life he might be. In May, Furtwängler wrote back that he regretted the unfortunate term he had used, and that he had meant only to contrast German orchestras as necessary articles in national life with American orchestras as luxury articles, which was a valid comparison. The fact that private sources had to support the existence of these groups he felt was a proof of his point of view: they were not considered essential enough to American cultural life to merit governmental subsidies and thus wider public support. He admitted, however, that the American private groups showed considerably more interest in their orchestras than Germans showed in theirs; he had not meant to cast aspersions on American orchestras, whose quality, he had realized while here, was far superior to that of their average German counterparts. It would have been well if Furtwängler had made a public statement for the American press, incorporating these views and clearing up the misunderstanding. He could have soothed some irritated feelings had he done so: but he did not choose to placate American opinion.

The next time Furtwängler's name appeared in American headlines was in a context no one could have foreseen when he had left New York in 1927, a political context which was to cloud his name until the present. It was in April 1933, shortly after Hitler came to power in Germany. Nazi pogroms had begun immediately, and countless Jewish and "undesirable" musicians, museum directors, members of the theatre world, artists, physicians, bankers, university professors, journalists, civil servants, and other representatives of the

VIENNA, 1930

REHEARSAL IN VIENNA, 1944

professions were dismissed from their posts. German musical life, in spite of the terrible difficulties of the inflation and Depression following the World War, now faced the greatest frontal attack in its history. Furtwängler had taken the Berlin Philharmonic on a tour of England, Holland and Belgium the day after Hitler came to power, and was consequently unaware of the extent of these dismissals in Germany. His first taste of what was to come was a threatened Nazi boycott of his concert in Bielefeld, on the way back to Berlin: on the train from Holland, an S.S. Officer had overheard his joking conversation against taxes with his Jewish secretary, Dr. Berta Geissmar, and had denounced both as "anti-National" criminals. Shortly thereafter, Hitler was sent a memorandum charging that Furtwängler, incited by his Jewish secretary, was depositing abroad the fees from his concerts there, and forcing the Orchestra to go without salary for months. These two incidents were only the beginning of many involving Miss Geissmar, against whom the Nazis waged a bitter struggle until she emigrated in 1935.

Furtwängler soon had an opportunity to see the "revolution" at work in the German cultural world. Adolf Busch had made it clear that he would no longer concertize in Germany, in protest against the Nazi decision that his friend and musical collaborator Rudolf Serkin was "intolerable." Max Reinhardt, the great stage director, went into exile, as did Otto Klemperer. In their attempts to force Bruno Walter to cancel a concert with the Leipzig Gewandhaus Orchestra, the Nazis tried to set fire to the Gewandhaus itself; Walter withdrew after the efforts of the Orchestra's Board to defend him proved futile. In Berlin, the Philharmonic concert agent Louise Wolff was telephoned by Walther Funk, then a State Secretary in Goebbels' Propaganda Ministry, and notified that if Walter appeared to conduct the concert she had arranged, "everything in the hall will be smashed to pieces."[1] Furtwängler was asked to replace Walter, but he refused. Walter soon went into exile; and Fritz Klein, the editor of the *Deutsche Allgemeine Zeitung*, the only newspaper daring to defend him, was dead a short time later. The Nazi press announced that he had fallen from a horse.

As a result of these incidents, Furtwängler addressed an Open Letter of protest to Goebbels on April 12; Goebbels published it, with a spurious "refutation," in the Nazi press:

"In view of the many years during which I have taken part in Germany's public life, and in view of my connection with German music, I am taking the liberty of attracting your attention to certain events which may, in my opinion, detract from the restitution of our national dignity, which we all welcome so gratefully and with such joy.

I speak entirely as an artist. It is the function of art and artists to unite and not to disrupt. I acknowledge only one ultimate difference: between good and bad art. But while a line of demarcation is drawn between Jews and non-Jews—even when the political attitude of the men concerned gives no cause for complaint—and this line is inexorable, the other important and decisive line of demarcation, that between good and bad art, is altogether neglected.

Today, musical life, weakened as it is by the world crisis and the radio, can stand no more experiments. One cannot fix quotas for music, as one can for other essentials, such as potatoes and bread. If nothing worth hearing is offered in concerts, people will simply stay away. For this reason the quality of music is not only an idealistic problem, but a matter of survival. If the fight against Jewry is directed chiefly against those artists who are themselves rootless and destructive, who seek to impress through trash and sterile virtuosity, this

---

[1] See Bruno Walter, *Theme and Variations* (New York, Alfred A. Knopf, 1946 and 1959), p. 298.

34

is only correct. The struggle against them and the spirit they personify—and this spirit also has its German devotees—cannot be waged vigorously and thoroughly enough. But when this attack is directed against real artists as well, it is not in the best interests of our cultural life. Real artists are very rare, and no country can afford to renounce their services without great damage to its culture.

It must, therefore, be said plainly that men like Walter, Klemperer, and Reinhardt and others must be enabled with their art to have their say in Germany in the future. I say again: let our fight be against the reckless, disintegrating, shallow, destructive spirit, but not against the real artist, who in his own way, however his art may be appraised, is always creative and thus constructive.

In this spirit I appeal to you in the name of German art lest things happen that can perhaps never be righted."[2]

In spite of the claptrap of Goebbels' "refutation"— "those of us who are creating modern German politics consider ourselves artists," ". . . art can be not only good or bad, but racially conditioned," "many German musicians during the past fourteen years had been condemned to silence by their Jewish rivals"—the fact that he published Furtwängler's letter in Germany meant that he allowed a voice for sanity to be raised from within, heard by a public severed from the outside world since the Nazis had come to power. Furtwängler was "inundated by congratulations, telegrams, and letters," as Miss Geissmar recalled.[3] Abroad, and in America, this

[2] This translation closely follows that of Margaret Goldsmith in Curt Riess's *Wilhelm Furtwängler* (London, Frederick Muller, 1955), pp. 102-3, and Berta Geissmar in her work *The Baton and the Jackboot* (London, Hamish Hamilton, 1944), pp. 78-9, with minor additions. The original German text may be found in Furtwängler's *Ton und Wort* (Wiesbaden, F. A. Brockhaus, 1954), pp. 70-1.

[3] Berta Geissmar, *op. cit.,* p. 80.

protest was welcomed and cheered; everyone awaited further protests from circles within the Third Reich. There were few. It was Furtwängler again who made the most famous of them.

What Americans could not know, for it never made the headlines, was that a constant battle between Furtwängler and Nazi officials was being waged behind the scenes. Miss Geissmar later reported in her memoirs:[4]

"As soon as the interferences with and encroachments on musical institutions began, he received masses of reports and desperate appeals for help. Everybody wrote to him about their troubles, and received replies promising the help he thought was his to give. Heads of concert associations arrived, artists begged for interviews and advice. Dismissed opera directors and broadcasting officials appeared to implore his aid. The files dealing with these cases form a most moving document of the early days of Nazi tyranny.

Furtwängler began to submit to the authorities individual cases that he deemed important. His requests were always most civilly received, but were passed from one authority to another. If he spoke to a high Government official, he was always promised an immediate settlement of the case. The fulfilment of the promise, however, was either cynically ignored or sabotaged by some underling. One soon learned that even the Minister was helpless if the subordinate bodies disagreed. Nevertheless, Furtwängler was untiring in his efforts. Day after day was passed in the attempts to contact officials and their staffs. All this was nerve-wracking to a sensitive artist. Once, when a minister who had asked him to telephone at a certain hour was still unavailable at the fourth attempt, Furtwängler angrily banged his fist through a window and hurt his hand. I got off with a splinter in my face."

---

[4] *Ibid.*, p. 78.

The loss of these files from the early days of the Nazi tyranny, in fact from the years until November 1943, in the partial destruction of the Berlin *Philharmonie*, means that one can never know how many cases Furtwängler fought out or how many lives he saved. Even if one did have them, they would not yield the entire story, because many decisions were made in personal or telephoned interviews. Miss Geissmar mentions the difficulty of dealing with the underlings in various Nazi ministries: these were more often than not crude and uneducated people, rewarded with their positions solely because of loyalty to the Nazi party, and belonging to the few in Germany for whom the name "Furtwängler" meant little. Many times in the next twelve years, Furtwängler, the world-renowned conductor, found himself with hat in hand in the waiting rooms of vain and stupid nobodies who might never have heard of him, who would see him when and if they pleased, whose whims could decide the fate of the man for whom he had come to plead. There is a revealing letter from Furtwängler on this subject, dated October 10, 1933, to Felix Lederer, an older Jewish colleague who had been placed under ban by the Nazis:

"Dear Lederer,

I am ready and willing at all times to intercede for you with fullest conviction. I suggest, however, that it would be better if I had some specific grounds or reason for this, because when it happens out of a clear sky, it could hurt more than help in certain circumstances. I never know what the mentality of the authorities will be. Perhaps you can send me further details, for example, how long your contract runs, etc."

Despite Furtwängler's intervention to have the ban lifted in 1933, Lederer was dismissed from his post as General Music Director in Saarbrücken when the Nazis took over the

Saar in 1935; to its great credit, the city insisted on continuing to pay his salary throughout the years of the Hitler régime. In 1941, Lederer was arrested in Berlin and taken to the Gestapo detention center in the Kleine Hamburger Strasse to await deportation to Auschwitz. Immediately his wife contacted Furtwängler, who was fortunately in Berlin at the time, and the next day Lederer was released. There is no contemporary correspondence about this intervention; it was swiftly carried out by other means.

At the end of 1933, during a particularly bitter Nazi press campaign against his "un-German" behavior in retaining Miss Geissmar as his secretary, Furtwängler was visited by twenty persons following a rehearsal with the Berlin Philharmonic in Cologne: Hermann Abendroth, the General Music Director in Cologne, had been dismissed by the Nazis and several professors from the Cologne Conservatory had been discharged with him. For two hours, almost until the beginning of the concert, Furtwängler listened to them all, one by one, and promised to do what he could. At the last moment, he hurriedly changed and mounted the podium. Later, after his intercession, Abendroth was appointed Conductor of the Leipzig Gewandhaus Orchestra. Testimony of his Berlin musicians shows that such scenes took place regularly after rehearsals and concerts, at home and on tour.

Other incidents of intervention were never committed to writing for reasons of danger, but in one of them at least, a record came to light after the war. In a letter to the *London Times* on December 21, 1946, one F. L. Kerran, referring to events in early 1939, wrote:

"While visiting the well-known Jewish teacher of singing, Dr. Walla Hess, who trained the famous singer Madame Hilde Konetzni, who this week sang in the Third Programme of the B.B.C. in *Die Walküre*, I heard a pupil of Mme. Hess, a young but very poor

Jewish youth whose magnificent voice greatly impressed me. This youth was 'on the run' and expected to be arrested at any moment by the Gestapo. I immediately got in touch with Dr. Furtwängler in Berlin, and he promised to help in any way he could. Within forty-eight hours he flew to Vienna from Berlin and saw and heard the boy and Mme. Hess at a secret rendezvous. Dr. Furtwängler gave me a letter as to the qualities of the boy's voice and his musical ability, and did the same for Mme. Hess. With these letters and the support of Sir Adrian Boult, the Home Office granted permission for both to come to this country.

Dr. Furtwängler indoubtedly took a grave personal risk in the service he rendered these two Jewish refugees."

It will be remembered how difficult for Jewish refugees entry into Great Britain was at this time.

Furtwängler intervened on several occasions for Siegmund von Hausegger, the conductor of the Munich Philharmonic, who was constantly under Nazi fire for his liberal sympathies. In 1933, he went to Berchtesgaden to plead the case of the violinist Carl Flesch, his old friend, before Hitler himself; years after this incident Flesch and his wife owed their escape from deportation to a concentration camp to Furtwängler. Another friend, Heinrich Wollheim, who had been dismissed from the Berlin State Opera Orchestra because he was half Jewish, was arrested for helping Germans and Jews escape to Switzerland from his home near Lake Constance; his wife asked Furtwängler's help, and Furtwängler went to see Himmler to obtain his release. Himmler refused, but Furtwängler managed to convince officials in the Goebbels Ministry that he needed Wollheim's assistance in copying scores; Wollheim was sent to Dachau, but was allowed to copy Furtwängler's scores, thus surviving the war. Other cases of Furtwängler's intervention were not so successful,

39

however. In 1942, he made all the necessary and difficult arrangements for the emigration of an elderly Jewish music critic in Vienna, one Frau Dr. Elsa Bienenfeld, to Switzerland; she was arrested at the frontier when gold buttons were found on her person, and never heard from again. The following year, Karlrobert Kreiten, a gifted young German pianist, was arrested by the Gestapo for remarking that "Hitler the carpet-biter" could never win the war; he was placed in solitary confinement at first, then transferred to the Moabit prison in Berlin to await trial for his "defeatist views." Furtwängler heard of the arrest from friends, and he assured a Security Police official that Kreiten was innocent; he was told that the prisoner would soon be released. Three months later the Kreiten family received an anonymous letter notifying them that Karlrobert had been sentenced to death by a People's Court; in spite of their frantic petitions he was executed, and a bill for his execution was sent to them, for payment within a week. Only then did Furtwängler learn what had happened. He wrote the Kreiten family:

> "I have heard with horror about the fate of Karlrobert Kreiten. . . . When, in the summer, I left Berlin, I believed as you, too, believed, that the affair had taken a turn for the better. And now this end! I assure you that I sympathize with your grief and share it. I well remember the last few times I heard him play. A real, genuine, and great hope has been buried. . . ."

Another young musician, Richard Geyer of Vienna, a fledgling composer, had been conscripted at eighteen for an army unit that was being used as cannon fodder. Furtwängler petitioned and telephoned the Propaganda Ministry to have the boy assigned to another unit. His pleas failed, and Geyer was killed shortly after arriving at the front. The Nazi official at the Ministry had laughed at Furtwängler's request when he telephoned.[5]

All these incidents of Furtwängler's intervention for Nazi victims were unknown abroad. The struggles with Nazi officialdom which never made the headlines were not limited to intervention for persons in trouble, however. The dismissal of Jewish conductors, soloists, composers and music coaches had meant that German musical life was suddenly filled with Nazi "stars," the musicians who Goebbels charged had been "condemned to silence by their Jewish rivals." Constant pressures were exerted on Furtwängler to engage them as co-conductors or soloists, to perform their compositions or to recommend them for new posts. He refused. All about him he saw the disintegration of German musical life: each week more soloists of international rank refused to appear in Germany, more German composers were banned, more musicians were dismissed from their posts, more critics muzzled by the Nazi press. On his next tour with the Philharmonic he found himself facing half-filled houses for the first time in his career: the Jews were intimidated and stayed away, and the Nazis often boycotted the Orchestra because Furtwängler had refused to "Aryanize" it. There was a particularly harsh incident in Mannheim.[6] Until the war, whenever he went on

---

[5] Curt Riess, *Wilhelm Furtwängler* (London, Frederick Muller, 1955), pp. 202-5.

[6] Cf. Louis P. Lochner in *Furtwängler Recalled,* ed. Daniel Gillis (Zürich, Atlantis Verlag and Tuckahoe, N. Y., John DeGraff, Inc., 1966), p. 82. A friend of Furtwängler's mother, Margaret Kolmar, an émigrée in Berkeley, California, recently recounted Furtwängler's visit to Baden with his Orchestra at this time: "Furtwängler insisted on my going to his concert, though I told him that my husband and I never went out any more, because we did not wish to mingle with Nazis. He insisted, and I went with my then ten-year-old son Klaus. We were sitting with old Mrs. Furtwängler in the first row, and it was a great shock to me to sit next to the Gauleiter of Baden. Furtwängler found it rather amusing, and even wanted me to come to the reception afterwards at a hotel. It showed me then how far away he was from the evil politics of the times. Later he wanted to give us introductory letters to friends

tour abroad, he was visited by Jewish exiles from Germany who came to him for help and advice. Andrew Schulhof, his friend who emigrated to New York, later recalled to him in November 1945:

> "I remember that you gave or sent every last pfennig you earned abroad and could make mobile, to your needy friends in exile, and that you were often warned that this offense was punishable by death. I remember in particular how you nearly missed the train in the Hague on February 1, 1939, because you were still writing out money orders to them."

In June 1933, the American press noted with approval that Furtwängler had won his fight to retain his Jewish musicians in the Berlin Philharmonic in defiance of a new law to "Aryanize" all orchestras. The next month his name appeared in the headlines as a result of another test case. In order to combat the disintegration of German musical life, Furtwängler reasoned that if internationally renowned soloists, some of them Jewish, could be persuaded to appear in Berlin again, the German provincial cities would have a precedent to support their efforts to engage and retain other, less famous Jewish musicians. Accordingly, for the 1934-5 Philharmonic season, he invited Pablo Casals, Alfred Cortot, Josef Hofmann, Bronislaw Huberman, Fritz Kreisler, the young Yehudi Menuhin, Gregor Piatigorsky, his former First Cellist in the Philharmonic, Jacques Thibaud and Artur Schnabel. "Someone must make a beginning to break down the wall that keeps us apart," he wrote. All the musicians felt that a restoration of freedom by the government of Germany must precede their reappearance before the German public. They praised Furtwängler's stand but doubted the

---

in England and America, but we did not accept this, as we did not wish to get him into any trouble."

intentions of the Nazis. All refused the invitations, though Cortot later reversed his decision and came to Berlin.

All German musicians were obliged to belong to the newly-organized Reich Music Chamber whose President was Richard Strauss, and Furtwängler cherished the naïve hope that he would increase his power to counteract the steady dissolution of German musical life by accepting appointment as Vice-President of this organization. He felt that in such a position he could take advantage of the peculiar German respect for titles and authority and thus not only have more to say about what went on in musical circles, but also be of more use to friends in political difficulties if he developed his connections with Nazi officials. For a time, things worked out as he hoped. But soon his open attempts at resistance led to a reversal. Miss Geissmar, who worked closely with him in all his dealings with the Chamber, wrote[7]

". . . He usually opposed everything, with the result that the bureaucracy, and last but not least, Strauss himself, began to conceal things from him. This constant and futile underground struggle gradually began to sap his nervous energy, yet he did not relax his efforts for the maintenance of his standards and wrote one memorandum after the other to demonstrate the shortcomings in every field. These memoranda were usually handed to the Minister in question directly. But as they naturally had to be filed, sometimes the very thing to be avoided actually happened: the papers fell into the hands of the underlings. It is significant that one of these documents dealing with the corruption in several departments and their chiefs, disappeared in the

---

[7] *The Baton and the Jackboot* (London, Hamish Hamilton, 1944), p. 139. Émigré historian Ernest K. Bramsted has recently written, "In those early days Goebbels was prepared to make concessions to the independent spirit of men like Furtwängler in order to retain their high prestige for the new régime." Cf. *Goebbels and National Socialist Propaganda 1925-1945* (East Lansing, Michigan State University Press, 1965), p. 65.

Ministry of Propaganda, and all that could be found was the empty file!

The underlings in official positions felt that their jobs were threatened by Furtwängler, and soon he had hardly any friends left in official quarters. . . ."

In July 1933 he was notified by telegraph that Goering had appointed him Prussian Councillor of State. This honorary title was being dispensed rather freely among prominent scientists, actors, artists, businessmen, even Social Democrats, and the purpose of the new Council was to make suggestions to the government on improvement of their own fields. Furtwängler attended one meeting. In early August 1933, as a result of the shocks sustained in recent months by the humiliations of its concert agency, Wolff and Sachs, and the loss of its large Jewish public, the Berlin Philharmonic found itself on the brink of financial disaster. Furtwängler went to see Hitler at Obersalzberg with a memorandum stating that unless its subsidies guaranteed by the Weimar Republic were enlarged, the Orchestra would be forced to disband; it also stated that in spite of this financial embarrassment, "Aryanization" of the Orchestra was out of the question. Miss Geissmar soon received a report of this meeting.[8]

"During their discussion of general and political matters, Hitler and Furtwängler shouted at each other for about two hours, and Furtwängler almost forgot the main subject—the Orchestra. He was so perturbed by the interview that he rang me up from Munich immediately afterwards, saying that he now understood what was at the bottom of Hitler's stubborn point of view. It was not the Jewish question alone, but his attitude, inimical to all intellectual matters. This telephone conversation—as we soon discovered—was tapped by the Nazis."

8 *Op. cit.,* p. 103.

44

In spite of the angry interview, the Philharmonic was given its subsidy and spared, for the time being, the threat of "Aryanization."

The next, and most dramatic, appearance of Furtwängler in the international press was his public defense of Paul Hindemith, the target of a relentless Nazi press campaign. His opera *Mathis der Maler* had been banned from production at the Berlin State Opera, which was under Furtwängler's Directorship according to a contract signed in the last days of the Weimar Republic; Furtwängler appealed for removal of the ban. His appeal was ignored. He programmed a Philharmonic performance of symphonic excerpts from the opera, and the work was received by the Berlin public with great enthusiasm. The Nazis, enraged by this success, which they correctly assessed as an anti-government demonstration, intensified their attacks on Hindemith. Furtwängler published his second Open Letter of protest, a detailed defense of Hindemith, in the *Deutsche Allgemeine Zeitung* of November 25, 1934, warning that if the campaign against the composer continued, he himself would resign all positions. The international press acclaimed this article, for it proved that, five months after the mass murders following the Ernst Röhm *"Putsch,"* a man still dared defy the Nazi government publicly. As in the case of the first Open Letter to Goebbels, however, though acclaimed by the world, this article too proved futile: a few days later Furtwängler resigned. In sympathy, Erich Kleiber resigned from the Berlin State Opera.

On December 7, 1934, the Berlin correspondent of the *London Times* reported:[9]

"Herr Alfred Rosenberg, who, as Herr Hitler's spe-

---

[9] See Percy A. Scholes, "The Nazi Regime and Music," *The Oxford Companion to Music,* Ninth Edition (London, Oxford University Press, 1960), pp. 400-1.

cial 'Supervisor of Intellectual Training' for the National-Socialist Party and head of the National-Socialist Culture Community, has more to say than any other single person in matters of art, political philosophy, and education, discusses today in the Nazi *Völkische Beobachter* (of which he is editor) the resignation of Herr Furtwängler from his three high musical appointments.

Herr Rosenberg's article shows clearly that Herr Furtwängler's unforgivable offense was to conduct the first performance of Herr Hindemith's new work (*Mathis the Painter*) and then, when this caused a violent conflict behind the scenes, to publish a spirited defense of Herr Hindemith as an artist.

'When a talented musician like Hindemith' (says Herr Rosenberg), 'after German beginnings, lives and works and feels himself at home in Jewish company; when he associates almost entirely with Jews; when he lends himself, in accordance with the spirit of the November Republic, to the worst kind of tawdry imitation of German music, then that is his own affair, but it gives others the right to shun him and his circle. A revolution has now removed the entire human, artistic, and political associations of Herr Hindemith.'

'It is deeply regrettable,' Herr Rosenberg continues, 'that so great an artist as Herr Furtwängler should have interfered in this dispute. But as he persisted in his "nineteenth-century ideas" and evidently had no further sympathy with "the great national struggle of our age," he took the consequences.' "

Months passed and no one in America heard what was happening to him; another hero had fallen, or so it seemed. There were rumors that Furtwängler would come to Philadelphia the following season for a guest engagement. In fact, Arthur Judson of the Columbia Concerts Corporation conducted secret negotiations in Europe through Hans W. Heinsheimer, then of Vienna, for guest engagements with both the New York Philharmonic-Symphony and the Philadelphia Orchestra. But Furtwängler's hesitations about leaving Germany, Nazi control of his mail and telegrams, and the capriciousness of authorities in Berlin hindered any successful results. In a letter of December 19, 1934, Heinsheimer revealed to Judson the weird atmosphere in which these negotiations were carried on: Furtwängler looked terrible—pale, nervous, grown ten years older since summer, when he had last seen him. He spoke anxiously, in a low voice. He told Heinsheimer that he had received only one cable from Judson; he could not answer, because his own situation was unclear. He said that he hoped he would have his freedom of movement again in two or three weeks, and that he would go immediately to his house in Switzerland. All his mail was censored, his telephone was under the control of the secret police. Heinsheimer added that Furtwängler had the personal disgrace of Reichskanzler Hitler, that the police had taken his passport and that none knew exactly if they gave it back to him.

The Berlin Philharmonic was desperate, he continued, and was trying to get him back. But everyone said that there was no possibility for him to return, even if he wished. Sooner or later, Furtwängler would have to leave Germany; but nobody knew the future, and the embarrassment of the authorities was understandable after Kleiber's resignation and subsequent refusal to return to the Berlin State Opera. Heinsheimer thought it possible that they attempt to get Furtwängler back in spite of all that happened. That, and the personal danger in which he lived might have been the reason why Furtwängler refused for the moment to make any decision for his projects abroad. Heinsheimer informed Judson that he had asked a clever and cautious friend in Berlin to maintain contact with Furtwängler. They had fixed a code, so that every letter might be overlooked by the police without danger. The name "Furtwängler" was never mentioned.

In Berlin Heinsheimer brought each letter personally to Furtwängler and waited personally for an answer. Heinsheimer himself was in contact with this friend through a third person in Vienna, so that letters and telephone calls were going to two different Viennese addresses. He assured Judson that this news was not a story by Edgar Wallace, with false addresses, secret police, etc., but the truth; a very serious and very dangerous business. He implored Judson to keep everything secret, adding that Judson had not seen the New Germany as he saw it on his monthly visits, and that one word in an American paper, one indiscretion, could risk Furtwängler's life.

The public here, of course, knew nothing of this. Then, suddenly, in April 1935, American readers were startled to see Furtwängler resume conducting in Berlin. Goebbels announced that[10]

> "The interview between Reichsminister Dr. Goebbels and Dr. Wilhelm Furtwängler, and the declaration made by Dr. Furtwängler in the course of this conversation, settled a conflict which has been detrimental to German music. It is no longer necessary to mention the origins of this conflict. Let it be said, however, that obviously Dr. Furtwängler himself underestimated the effects of his article which began the dispute. He thought that he could treat a musical problem—which, as is known, concerned Hindemith—from a purely artistic point of view, and in so doing he forgot that in the National State no issue is isolated. Furtwängler overlooked our totalitarian outlook, which is an integral part of National Socialism. We must honor him because he himself has now acknowledged, by his declaration, the restrictions, imposed by the State, which must be accepted by even the greatest musicians."

---

[10] Cf. Curt Riess, *Wilhelm Furtwängler* (London, Frederick Muller Ltd., 1955), pp. 145-6.

Goebbels did not publish Furtwängler's declaration itself, nor would Hitler later agree to publication. For the first time Furtwängler had acknowledged that the government was in control of all cultural policies, which had been a fact since January 1933. He was willing to return to German musical life as a Guest Conductor, without official posts of any kind, and without obligations or responsibilities of association in governmental cultural policies. These conditions of his statement were accepted, but the refusal of the government to publish them meant that many abroad saw Furtwängler's return to public life in Nazi Germany as a capitulation, a betrayal of his earlier courage. By some, it was assumed that Furtwängler had been restored to all positions, when in fact he held only one, the post of Councillor of State which could only be withdrawn by the government itself. This the government would not do; the title was too useful a device in associating Furtwängler with the régime.

Whatever the suppressed technicalities of the agreement, on April 25, 1935, the Berlin musical public roared its welcome for twenty-five minutes when Furtwängler appeared on the stage of the *Philharmonie* for his first concert since his resignation. The applause was both in protest for his humiliation by the government and in gratitude for his return. Louis P. Lochner later recalled this scene:

> "I remember it so distinctly because my wife and I sat in the same row with the British Ambassador, Sir Eric Phipps. The ovation which was given Furtwängler was so tremendous and so pronouncedly anti-Nazi that Sir Eric remarked to us, 'This is no longer a concert— it is a political demonstration!' Saying which, he resumed applauding loudly."

When the audience had quieted down, Furtwängler led his Philharmonic in the *Egmont Overture,* the *Pastorale* and

Fifth Symphonies of Beethoven. When the last crashing chords of the *Fifth* had sounded, the audience again broke into a wild demonstration for him, this time lasting an hour.

The demand for a repeat concert was so great that one was scheduled for May 5. Shortly before Furtwängler appeared, Hitler strode in with several members of his entourage. The audience was surprised and confused as the group occupied seats in the front row; there was a scattering of applause from the Nazis already present. When Furtwängler emerged from the wings, a thunderous ovation greeted him. Engulfed by the frantic applause for Furtwängler, Hitler at first blushed, then accepted the situation and began applauding. Furtwängler was photographed bowing, both hands by his sides, as Hitler and his friends did so. This photograph was used in America after the war as "proof of Furtwängler's Nazi connections" by circles which knew nothing of the electrifying atmosphere of this concert. They overlooked the crucial point of the photograph: Furtwängler had refused to raise his right arm in the obligatory Nazi salute. This was an affront of the first order to Hitler and his minions. When the concert had ended, another demonstration erupted and continued long after Hitler and his party had left the hall.

III

IN EARLY 1936, when Toscanini decided to retire as Musical Director of the Philharmonic-Symphony Orchestra of New York, he recommended that the Board engage Furtwängler to take his place. Furtwängler, in Vienna at the time, was hesitant. He knew that his decision to resume conducting in Germany the previous year had cost him many friends in America, thus opening the possibility for resistance to his coming; and he was reluctant to leave the country where he felt he belonged. But he stated his willingness to come to New York if he was allowed to continue conducting in Germany and Europe, insofar as this would be compatible with his New York season. This proposal was acceptable to the Board, provided Furtwängler held no other official conducting post in Germany or elsewhere. An agreement was made, and his appointment was announced on February 28, 1936.

Almost immediately word came from Berlin that Furtwängler had been reinstated as Director of the Berlin State Opera. Furtwängler was by now en route from Vienna to Egypt, and it was impossible for the Philharmonic Board to reach him at once for clarification. In Berlin, inquiries by

The Associated Press, which had reported the State Opera appointment, resulted in its affirmation by official sources. Jewish circles in New York, though they included many of Furtwängler's former audience, could not understand why he had chosen to remain in Germany if he was not a Nazi; they were convinced that this new appointment in Berlin proved his good relations with the Nazis; he was, after all, a German product and should be boycotted like any other German product; and they resented the fact that the Philharmonic post had been offered to him rather than to Bruno Walter or Otto Klemperer, both victims of Nazi persecution.

On March 1, the newspapers carried a public protest against Furtwängler's engagement by Ira A. Hirschmann, former member of the Philharmonic Board, and Rev. Dr. Stephen S. Wise. Letters for and against the appointment began to appear in the newspaper columns. When the Board established contact with Furtwängler in Egypt and inquired about the Berlin appointment he wired back that he was not the Director of the Berlin State Opera. The Board published his cable and issued an accompanying statement on March 7.

> "From reports in the public press, an impression has been given that the appointment of Mr. Furtwängler has a national or racial significance.
>
> There is no foundation whatever for any such representation. The appointment was promoted solely by artistic considerations, and because the directors, with Maestro Toscanini's approval, believe that Mr. Furtwängler, one of the foremost of living conductors, is a leader so equipped to arouse great interest among New York music lovers.
>
> He has lately served as conductor in Vienna, Budapest, London, Paris and Warsaw and other important musical centers of Europe. Wherever he has appeared he has aroused the greatest interest and acclaim.
>
> He comes here in a similar capacity.

Any attempt to make it appear that this engagement involves any recognition of the Nazi dictatorship or any approval of its artistic policies is unwarranted and misleading. It is well to bring to the attention of those who support music that Mr. Furtwängler risked and sacrificed his prominent position in Germany by waging single-handed, earnestly and persistently, a contest for tolerance or broadmindedness toward musicians as well as composers."

The statement was signed by Clarence H. Mackay, Marshall Field, Charles Triller, Felix Warburg, Walter W. Price, Edwin T. Rice, Richard W. G. Welling, and Arthur Judson, executive secretary.

But on the day this statement was printed in the newspapers, March 7, an event occurred which made the Board's stubborn persistence hopeless. In violation of treaty obligations, Hitler occupied the Rhineland. Anti-German sentiment was very strong in New York and the controversy over the appointment grew more severe. On March 9, announcement was made of the formation of a committee by Ira A. Hirschmann, in order to convince the Board to withdraw the appointment by threatening boycott and mass cancellation of subscriptions. The American Federation of Musicians, the Teachers' Union, the American Federation of Labor and various trade unions protested. The German-American Bund threatened not to let Furtwängler land if he came. This was a strange addition to the alliance. Unknown to Jewish and liberal circles in America, Goering had sought Furtwängler's services as Director of the Berlin State Opera for many months and, after Furtwängler's repeated refusals, had violently objected to Furtwängler's accepting the New York offer. His false announcement of the State Opera appointment was designed to add fuel to anti-Furtwängler sentiment in New York and thus make the appointment there untenable.

The Jewish and liberal groups in New York unwittingly played into Goering's hands; the Bund, however, taking its cue from Berlin, knew exactly what it was doing when it protested.

On March 15, the Philharmonic Board published Furtwängler's withdrawal by cable:

> "Political controversy disagreeable to me. Am not politician but exponent of German music which belongs to all humanity regardless of politics. I propose to postpone my season in the interest of the Philharmonic Society until the time public realizes that politics and music are apart. If quote press quote verbatim."

The Philharmonic Board issued a formal statement at the same time.

> "While confirming the position taken in a signed statement of March 7, the executive committee of the Society feels it must regretfully accede to the wishes expressed in the above cable, although it involves the loss to New York of one of the foremost conductors of the world. Mr. Furtwängler's selection as conductor was actuated by no other consideration than the highest musical interests of the orchestra and its public. The executive committee is credibly informed that Mr. Furtwängler has not been a member of any political party in Germany and it greatly deplores the political implications that have been read into the appointment."

This statement, however, did not deter *Time* from celebrating the withdrawal in an article entitled, "Nazi Stays Home."

Thus America lost Furtwängler once again. Throughout the controversy Toscanini had refrained from defending his choice of a successor. He saw Furtwängler some months later in Paris and criticized him for not having fought more resolutely to come to New York. At Salzburg in summer

1937, Toscanini broke with Furtwängler. He was irritated that Furtwängler had been invited to conduct at the Festival because he was also conducting at Bayreuth after an absence of five years, and had declared that he himself would not appear in Salzburg. There are various accounts of the break. Howard Taubman in his 1951 biography of Toscanini, provided the following:[1]

> "After listening to much pleading, Toscanini agreed to return to Salzburg on two conditions—that he would not have to see or have anything to do with Furtwängler and that Furtwängler would never again be asked back.
>
> One day Furtwängler walked into Toscanini's dressing room. As the maestro recalled the meeting years later, he smiled at the way the German, though he towered over him, seemed to be afraid of him.
>
> Toscanini glared at Furtwängler and said, "I don't want to see you."
>
> "Why?"
>
> "Because you're a Nazi."
>
> "It is not true," Furtwängler protested.
>
> "Yes, you are," Toscanini insisted, "Whether you have a party card or not. In London you lunch with Jews to make a good case for yourself so that you won't lose your position in the West. In Germany, you work for Hitler."
>
> Toscanini turned his back on the tall man, who slowly walked away."

Furtwängler gave a radically different account of this last meeting,[2] which took place not in Toscanini's dressing room but on the street.

> "Toscanini declared that, in his opinion, Furtwängler should not be permitted to return to Salzburg. 'In the

[1] *The Maestro* (New York, Simon and Schuster), p. 217.
[2] Curt Riess, *Wilhelm Furtwängler* (London, Frederick Muller, 1955), pp. 168-9.

world of today, it is impossible for a musician who conducts in an enslaved country to do so in a free country. If you conduct in Bayreuth, you should not conduct in Salzburg.'

Furtwängler replied: 'I am the same man I was six months ago when you reproached me for not accepting your invitation to come to New York.'

Toscanini said: 'Those were different times. Today there is only either—or.'

Furtwängler answered: 'I should be quite willing to give up coming to Salzburg, if this meant that your activities here would continue. Personally I believe that there are no enslaved and free countries. Human beings are free wherever Wagner and Beethoven are played, and if they are not free at first, they are freed while listening to these works. Music transports them to regions where the Gestapo can do them no harm.'

Toscanini was silent, and Furtwängler continued: 'If I conduct great music in a country which is, by chance, ruled by Hitler, must I therefore represent him? Does not great music, on the contrary, make me one of his antagonists? For is not great music utterly opposed to the soullessness of Nazism?'

Toscanini shook his head, he could not agree. 'Everyone,' he said, 'who conducts in the Third Reich is a Nazi!'

Furtwängler emphatically denied this. 'By that,' he said, 'you imply that art and music are merely propaganda, a false front, as it were, for any Government which happens to be in power. If a Nazi Government is in power, then, as a conductor, I am a Nazi; under the communists, I would be a communist; under the democrats, a democrat. . . . No, a thousand times, no! Music belongs to a different world, above chance political events!'

Toscanini shook his head. 'I disagree!' he said, and that ended the discussion which had lasted only a few minutes."

One wonders what gave Toscanini the idea that Austria was a free country after 1934.[3]

When Austria was annexed to Germany in 1938, friends from musical circles in Vienna appealed to Furtwängler to help prevent the Nazification of Austrian musical life. The Goebbels Ministry had begun immediately to extend its influence into all phases of Austrian culture, with the object of reducing Vienna to the status of a German provincial town. The Vienna Philharmonic was ordered to disband, and its Executive Committee, with the support of Gauleiter Joseph Bürckel, a personal enemy of Goebbels, requested Furtwängler to intervene. He agreed to accept an informal advisory post for musical affairs in Vienna, without contract or salary, in order to frustrate the plans of the Goebbels Ministry in Berlin. He succeeded in preventing the dissolution of the Philharmonic, and in protecting members of the Orchestra who were partly Jewish or had Jewish wives. He blocked the confiscation of the library owned by the Society of the Friends of Music and managed to preserve the identity of

[3] ". . . On February 12, 1934, seventeen thousand government troops and fascist militia had turned artillery on the workers' flats in Vienna, killing a thousand men, women and children and wounding three or four thousand more. Democratic political freedom was stamped out and Austria thereafter was ruled first by Dollfuss and then by Schuschnigg as a clerical-fascist dictatorship. It was certainly milder than the Nazi variety, as those of us who worked in both Berlin and Vienna in those days can testify. Nevertheless it deprived the Austrian people of their political freedom and subjected them to more repression than they had known under the Hapsburgs in the last decades of the monarchy. The author has discussed this more fully in *Midcentury Journey*.", William L. Shirer, *The Rise and Fall of the Third Reich, A History of Nazi Germany* (New York, Simon and Schuster, 1960), p. 325.

Taubman reports in his biography (p. 212) that "When Chancellor Engelbert Dolfuss was assassinated, Toscanini considered it a grave privilege to be invited to conduct the Verdi Requiem in his memory" in Vienna. Toscanini's last conducting appearance in fascist Italy had been in 1931, nearly a decade after the end of Italian political freedom, and he continued to visit his homeland through the summer of 1939. He had himself been a fascist candidate for public office in 1919 (cf. Dennis Mack Smith, *Italy, A Modern History* (2nd. ed., Ann Arbor, University of Michigan Press, 1969), p. 324).

the Vienna State Opera. This lobbying for Vienna in Berlin was very difficult, because it was carried on at a time when Furtwängler was the object of a hostile press campaign inspired by the Goering Ministry after his refusal to accept the Directorship of the Berlin State Opera in 1938.[4]

In the late thirties, Furtwängler was better understood in Western Europe than in America. In 1937 he was invited to share the planning of the British Coronation Season with Sir Thomas Beecham, a high honor for a foreigner. The French public admired his refusal to conduct the Nazi national anthem the *Horst Wessel Lied*, before a Berlin Philharmonic concert during the Paris World's Fair that same year. In summer 1939, when Franco-German relations were increasingly tense and inimical, the French Government appointed him Commander of the Legion of Honor. Hitler forbade publication of this fact in the Nazi press. Soon thereafter, the outbreak of the Second World War separated Furtwängler from his audiences abroad.

---

[4] See pp. 69 ff. below.

IV

THE END OF THE WAR found Furtwängler a refugee in Switzerland. Though in poor health, he was anxious to return to his homeland and help rebuild musical life there. In June 1945 he sent a resumé of his years under the Nazi régime to the American Legation in Berne. Two months later Gerald M. Mayer of the Press Department at the Legation replied:

> "I have just returned from Frankfurt where a conference was held by the competent authorities of the American Zone of Occupation. The Information Control Division has no objection to your return to Germany, where you would have to work out your own future. In other words, the Information Control Division would consider your privately engaging in activities in your own field, and you would have to apply for a license from them. As far as the Information Control Division was concerned, they would not be interested in availing themselves of your services at this time."

Travel between Switzerland and Germany was severely restricted, Berlin was in chaos, postal service was not yet reestablished, telegraph and telephone communications had been requisitioned by the Allied military governments. Furtwängler was unable to go to Berlin, and his Orchestra began its reorganization without him. Leo Borchard, its first postwar conductor, was shot by an American patrol in August 1945,[1] and the young Rumanian pianist Sergiu Celibidache, resident in Berlin, took over the Philharmonic. Famous conductors were not easily found; most had been placed under ban by the Western Allies pending investigation of their wartime activities.

In spite of primitive communications with Germany, friends and friends of friends somehow managed to send or bring news to Furtwängler in Clarens concerning events in Berlin. On December 12, 1945, he wrote his friend Andrew Schulhof, then a concert agent in New York, that he had been told his name was on the American black list. His case had originally been given to General Eisenhower, who was said to have decided to rehabilitate Furtwängler but later reversed his decision. In this same letter Furtwängler interpreted this Allied attitude:

"The entire problem can only be understood in a political sense. It is not at all a question of having definite evidence against me, for there is none, but the reason is that, within my modest circle, I was a type of 'representative man' for Germany long before Nazism and have remained so even under it. The Allies do not want such a man in Germany right now. I myself think that this policy is psychologically quite erroneous: it is directed against the very ones with whom the Allies should coöperate. In my own case, it may mean enforced retirement for several years. At the moment, I

---

[1] Given the post by the Soviets in early May, 1945, Borchard was a Moscow-born German whose career had been curtailed by the Nazis before the war. He was a member of the resistance group known as the "Uncle Emils," whose story is told by Ruth Andreas-Friedrich in her *Berlin Underground* 1938-1945 (New York, Henry Holt and Company, 1947), which is dedicated to his memory. The fatal incident is described by Joel Sayre in his Introduction to this book (p. xi).

myself see only one possibility: to inform the public in America, which—thank God—is still a democracy."

Unknown to Furtwängler at the time of writing was the fact that Yehudi Menuhin was attempting to do precisely this in New York. Menuhin had followed American troops into Paris in August 1944 and had there heard from French musicians how Furtwängler had resisted pressures from the Nazis to conduct in occupied Paris; even more impressive to him were the emphatic statements of the musicians that they would welcome Furtwängler in Paris immediately, an honor reserved for him alone among Germans. Menuhin had reported these statements in America in November 1944 and no opposing voice was raised. But in December 1945 it was quite different. In the months after the war ended he had been in all parts of Germany, had played for the survivors of Hitler's death camps, and had heard from some of them more reports of Furtwängler's intervention for Jewish musicians during the Third Reich. He announced these findings in a press conference when he returned, and almost immediately found himself the target of attack. Ira A. Hirschmann was again the spokesman of resistance.

"Menuhin chooses a rather critical moment in history to suggest the return of one of the Nazi satellites. . . . That it should be suggested for Furtwängler to return to America to purge his strain is so incredible as to be unthinkable. . . . We are enraged at the very thought of this Nazi invading America!"

Menuhin answered at once.

"Hirschmann misrepresented and misstated me. I never mentioned that Furtwängler should come to this country. . . . It is wrong to mention Furtwängler and those beasts on trial in Nüremberg in the same breath. It is

61

a very easy and cheap way of raising mass feelings. Even those beasts are getting a fair, democratic trial. Surely it is wrong to condemn Furtwängler, about whom there are divided opinions, without a fair trial."

He also criticized Hirschmann, in another interview, for "taking it upon himself to speak for the American people." Hirschmann was not disturbed by rebuttal, still less inclined to refrain from misstatements. On December 11 he told the *New York Herald Tribune:*

"As a former Attaché of the State Department during the War I was in possession of evidence which proved beyond any doubt the insoluble tie of Furtwängler with the Nazi leaders. Furtwängler was rated an official of the Third Reich. This information was available to me but was too well known by everyone to labor the point."

A reference to "evidence which proved beyond any doubt" Furtwängler's guilt, suggesting at first that as a State Department Attaché Hirschmann had access to documents unavailable otherwise. But the information, he added, was in the public domain—thus unwittingly conceding that he knew no more than anyone else. Though a State Department official, even on a temporary and informal basis,[2] Hirschmann seemed unaware of Furtwängler's resignation of all posts in 1934, and the nature of the office of "Prussian Councillor of State" from which he was not allowed to

---

[2] See Hirschmann's *Life Line to a Promised Land* (New York, The Vanguard Press, Inc., 1946); "I Made a Deal With Eichmann" in *Look* (May 9, 1961); his autobiography, *Caution to the Winds* (New York, David McKay, Inc., 1962); and Arthur D. Morse, *While Six Million Died, A Chronicle of American Apathy* (New York, Random House, 1968), pp. 314-21, 356-8 etc. Morse's book, as well as the more recent work by David S. Wyman, *Paper Walls. America and the Refugee Crisis 1938-1941* (Amherst, Mass., University of Massachusetts Press, 1968), ably chronicle the official and public disinterest here in the fate of Jewish refugees.

resign. He gave another statement to the *New York Daily Mirror* that same day:

> "I began fighting Furtwängler back in 1936, when he was signed to conduct the New York Philharmonic. We learned that he had signed a contract with the Hitler régime and we rejected him. We spared him embarrassment by allowing him to assert his health would be affected by arduous duties both here and abroad."

There are several errors here. In 1936 Furtwängler had denied that any contract with the German government existed; the Philharmonic Board accepted Furtwängler's denial and refused to drop him as Musical Director in spite of protests led by Hirschmann himself; the "we" is misleading, as Hirschmann was no longer a member of the Philharmonic Board in March 1936; the Board did not "spare Furtwängler embarrassment" by allowing him to give such excuses; no such assertion was ever made by Furtwängler; his health was good at that time; his musical commitments in Germany in 1936 were minimal, in fact he was devoting considerable time to composition. In spite of these errors Hirschmann expressed similar views in the *Herald Tribune* as well:

> "Mr. Menuhin's statement that Furtwängler declined the offer to become conductor of the New York Philharmonic Orchestra in 1936 is also not true. He was summarily rejected when it was learned that he simultaneously had a contract with the Hitler régime and the New York Philharmonic. In favor of the Philharmonic management it must be said that it was quick to see that it had made a fundamental error and withdrew the contract."

None bothered to check Hirschmann's claims.[3] Some of the

---

[3] For a more truthful but still somewhat inaccurate account of Hirschmann's bitter struggle with the Philharmonic Board over the Furtwängler

press was equally imprecise. *P M* reported that Furtwängler, after resigning his posts in 1934, was reinstated as Guest Conductor of the Berlin State Opera on March 1, 1935, and as Opera Director on September 3, 1935. Neither statement was true. Similar "facts" appeared in articles in *Music News* and *Musical America*. Hans W. Heinsheimer wrote Furtwängler from New York that the air had not yet cleared there; even Menuhin's views, he felt, came too soon after the war. Two weeks later, however, he sent a pro-Furtwängler article by Kurt List, editor of *Listen* magazine, with the comment that List had received several letters from readers, all in the affirmative. Furtwängler was not cheered by the news. Andrew Schulhof had written him on December 5, the day that Menuhin made his first statements, that "there are countless others, such as Primrose, Casadesus, Francescatti, and many of my friends who play an important role here and who I know will all be glad to take a stand for you." Not one voice was raised to help Menuhin. This silence from Furtwängler's famous "friends" in American musical circles, even from those who owed their careers to him, was to last until the end of his life. Schulhof himself, in October 1945, had promised to begin a newspaper campaign based on factual information Furtwängler had sent to him, but nothing ever came of it.

At home Furtwängler had even greater cause for disappointment. In February 1946, an official ban on his conducting activities in the Western Occupation Zones was announced by General John McClure of the American Informa-

appointment, see his *Caution to the Winds* (New York, David McKay Company, Inc., 1962), pp. 94-100. In this work Hirschmann still believes that Furtwängler was "First State Conductor" of the Berlin State Opera in 1936. He refers to an article by William Henderson of the *New York Sun* at that time, concerning the "elephant-hide insensitivity of the Board" in choosing Furtwängler, without mentioning that the Board was acting on the recommendation of his friend Toscanini.

WITH ISAAC STERN, LUCERNE, 1948

VIENNA, 1950

tion Control Division, who charged that Furtwängler had been "a tool of the Nazi party," that he had "lent an aura of respectability to the party," and had "remained in its good graces until its collapse." Unknown to Furtwängler, Menuhin had wired General McClure immediately:

"Unless you have secret incriminating evidence against Furtwängler supporting your accusation that he was a tool of Nazi party, I beg to take violent issue with your decision to ban him. The man never was a party member, held no official permanent conducting post following his resignation of Berlin Philharmonic Directorship in 1934 forfeiting thereby state pensions and support. Upon numerous occasions risked his own safety and reputation to plead for, help, and protect friends and colleagues. Do not believe that the fact of remaining in one's own country particularly when fulfilling a job of this nature more akin to a spiritual Red Cross or minister's mission is alone sufficient to condemn a man. On the contrary as a military man you would know that remaining at one's post often requires greater courage than running away. He saved, and for that we are deeply his debtors, the best part and only salvageable part of his own German culture. As for quote 'lending an aura of respectability to the party' end quote, are we the Allies not infinitely more guilty, and of our own free will, by recognizing and pactizing with these monsters until the last minute when almost despite ourselves we were literally dragged and unchivalrously knocked into this struggle, except of course for Great Britain which declared war before being directly attacked. Remember Munich and Berchtesgaden and all the years when we all wantonly abandoned to their cruel fate every brave and hopeful heart, every valiant and defiant nation. I believe it patently unjust and most cowardly for us to make of Furtwängler a scapegoat for our own crimes. If the man is guilty of specific crimes, accuse him and convict him. As far as I can see it is no punishment to be banned from sordid, filthy Berlin, and if the man now old and ill is willing and anxious to return to his exacting task and responsibilities, he should be encouraged, for that is where he belongs, right in Berlin. If this diseased nation should ever grow up to become a self-respecting member of the community of nations, it will be due to the efforts of men like Furtwängler who have proven that they are able to rescue from the war at least part of their soul. Witness the Berlin Philharmonic. These men alone are able to build on this unsullied base a better society. It is not by stifling such men that you will achieve your aim. Quite the contrary you will only stir up a justifiable resentment against a vandalism as real as the more obvious variety which carves up churches and paintings, and a resentment in which will join the outraged voices of musicians, colleagues, writers and men of integrity the world over regardless of nationality or creed including yours truly Yehudi Menuhin."

In Vienna, Furtwängler himself asked the émigré correspondent Curt Riess, who had a priority flight to Berlin pending, to show certain additional documents concerning his wartime activities to General McClure. Riess did so, and General McClure summoned him a few days later, stating that a mistake had been made and that the ban would be lifted "in a few weeks' time." The Russians offered Furtwängler the Directorship of the State Opera in their sector of Berlin, but under advisement of General McClure he agreed to await rehabilitation in the American sector where his Philharmonic was located.

In Vienna the Austrian Government was conducting its own investigation of Furtwängler's activities and recommended his rehabilitation in March 1946. This recommendation was ignored by the American Military Government. The "few weeks' time" of General McClure's promise dragged on into eighteen months, long after most of Furtwängler's colleagues had resumed conducting. In June 1946, a commission was set up by the Allies in Berlin to investigate Furtwängler.

This second commission also recommended Furtwängler's immediate rehabilitation. The Information Control Division dropped the recommendation, and proposed to turn the case over to the Denazification Commission. There was no legal justification for this: Denazification proceedings were intended for former members of the Nazi party seeking employment, and Furtwängler should not have come under their jurisdiction. Months passed. Contrary to Menuhin's expectation of protests from artists after the ban, Furtwängler's musical colleagues were conspicuously absent—with the exception of himself and Ernest Ansermet. Artur Schnabel advised Furtwängler to make no efforts whatsoever to publicize his side of the case, particularly in America, and to accept the fact that he would not conduct abroad for several years. In Switzerland, the left-wing press kept up an insistent attack against him, in spite of the public defense of Ansermet. Furtwängler had not held a baton in his hand for well over a year; his energies were directed into composition of his *Second Symphony*. Spending the summer in Clarens with his family, Furtwängler wrote to Fritz Zweig, a former colleague then living in Los Angeles, concerning these developments:

> "The results of the investigations are not being published, due to pressures from New York; all sorts of charges which have long since been refuted in the two inquiries, turn up again and again in the Allied-controlled press; and so I am being prevented from conducting in Germany and the rest of the world. Who is *really* interested in this situation? That is the question one is forced to ask oneself."

Curt Riess later recalled these months of waiting in Berlin:[4]

---

[4] *Wilhelm Furtwängler* (London, Frederick Muller Ltd., 1955), pp. 216-18. Estimates of the Information Control Division have not been friendly: see Harold Zink, *American Military Government in Germany* (New York,

"In the meantime his denazification has been postponed again and again. The chief objections—that, at least, was clear—came from the Americans, and this, in view of my conversations with General McClure, was positively grotesque. . . . It was a paradox. For while the Americans were continuously postponing a settlement of the Furtwängler case, individual Americans approached me and asked me to do what I could for Furtwängler. . . . The summer of 1946 was passing, and no one yet knew when Furtwängler would be denazified. I was still being asked to soothe him and to urge him not to conclude any agreement with the Russians . . . Nevertheless, it seemed unfair to ask a man supported in Switzerland by helpful and generous friends, to refuse appointments and engagements when no alternatives were being offered him. In the middle of November 1946, while I was in Berlin, I asked the American officer responsible for the denazification of musicians: 'When will Furtwängler's case be heard?' 'We don't know,' he said, 'It may take some time . . . perhaps six months or a year.' 'I can't,' I replied, 'with a clear conscience, put Furtwängler off any longer. On the contrary, I shall advise him to accept the next offer he has, even if it should be from the Russians!' I wrote accordingly to Furtwängler, but the letter was never posted, for forty-eight hours later the American officer telephoned to me: 'I am happy to inform you that Furtwängler's case is next on the list of the Denazification Tribunal in the Schlüter Strasse.' "

In America, late in 1946 when reports of Furtwängler's impending Denazification were printed, some of Furtwängler's

The Macmillan Company, 1947), 160-64, and Joseph Dunner, "Information Control in the American Zone of Germany 1945-1946," in *American Experiences in Military Government in World War II*, edited by Carl J. Friedrich (Ney York, Rinehart & Company, Inc., 1948), 276-91. John Gimbel's recent book *The American Occupation of Germany. Politics and the Military 1945-1949* (Stanford, Calif., Stanford University Press, 1968) unfortunately does not deal with cultural matters.

loyal émigré friends began to act. Fritz Zweig sent him a generally favorable article from *Life* written by Winthrop Sargent, and wrote that a group had been formed to help him. Friedelinde Wagner, Gilbert Back, former First Violinist of the Berlin Philharmonic, Alicia Ehlers, Ernst Gottlieb, and several others began a search for those German and Austrian Jewish refugees in America whose escape from the Nazis Furtwängler had made possible. An article was planned for *Musical America*. Dr. Hugo Strelitzer of Los Angeles, whose life Furtwängler had saved in August 1933, sent Zweig an affidavit giving details of his release from a Nazi prison; Professor Robert Hernried of Detroit sent a similar affidavit. Zweig wrote *Life* about Furtwängler's intervention for release of his nephew from Dachau in 1938; and other affidavits were assembled. They were not sent to Furtwängler in time to help him: in early December 1946, he was notified that he must appear for trial in Berlin later in the month. He travelled to Berlin by American military train, to face the Denazification court without advance briefing of the charges or benefit of legal counsel—the standard procedure in such trials.[5]

Once again the "Furtwängler case" was discussed in the American press, in greater detail than ever before. The fullest treatment was in the *Times* of December 29, 1946, by Delbert Clark, entitled "Furtwängler's Standards on Trial in Berlin." It will be reproduced here in its entirety, and each of its many distortions and misstatements will be corrected in order.

"On Tuesday, December 17, 1946, Wilhelm Furtwängler was acquitted of Nazi activities by the Berlin denazification tribunal. It was a great day for Dr. Furt-

---

[5] See Constantine Fitzgibbon's helpful study, *Denazification* (New York, W. W. Norton & Company Inc., 1969).

wängler if one is not too precise in appraising moral values. The tribunal acquitted him on the ground of insufficient evidence but, perhaps unwittingly, convicted him of another offense which is not punishable under any modern law.

That offense was in the same general category as those committed by Beniamino Gigli in Italy and Richard Strauss in Austria; the offense of so overlooking moral values and fixed principles that he was able and willing to make maximum use of a régime which he alleged was obnoxious to him, to maintain himself in a position of comfort and security and to kick down any potential competitors for that position. Positive Nazi activity is punishable under the rules of these tribunals; lack of moral sense is not yet a crime."

The moralizing accents of the opening sentences, with their appeal to "higher laws," clearly establish the writer's position: no evidence conflicting with his *a priori* assumptions is included in his following paragraphs.

"In his trial, which lasted two full days, the proved charges were that Dr. Furtwängler, who used to be acclaimed as Germany's greatest orchestra conductor, had been honorary Prussian State Councillor appointed by Hermann Goering, and that he continued as President of the Berlin Music Chamber and director of the Berlin Philharmonic Orchestra during part of the Hitler régime. Charges not proved were that he had been intimate with the Ministry of Propaganda, if not with Goebbels himself, and had used that intimacy to procure punishment for a Berlin critic who dared praise Herbert von Karajan, young guest conductor, at his expense.

"As for proved charges, Dr. Furtwängler said it was obviously impossible to resign as Prussian State Councillor since Goering had appointed him and Goering alone could remove him. And he had eventually resigned both musical directorates.

"He contended he had quit these positions as a

result of arguments with Goebbels over the retention of Jewish musicians. But the former business manager of the Philharmonic who appeared as a defense witness and who had not heard Furtwängler's testimony, did him a disservice by saying that the conductor was unable to continue administrative jobs because of the pressure of guest engagements outside Germany. There appears to be little question that he had indeed protected some Jewish musicians, whether for reasons of personal friendship or because of opposition to the Nazi régime is unclear. However, when it is said of a German 'Some of his best friends were Jews,' it is often taken as proof positive that he was no Nazi."

Only one of the three "proved charges" was in fact a charge at all. Furtwängler had never been President of the Berlin Music Chamber, which indeed never existed. He had been Vice-President of the Reich Music Chamber, the organization to which all German musicians were obliged to belong, and had publicly resigned in November 1934. The fact that he directed the Berlin Philharmonic Orchestra as its Permanent Conductor was not held against him: it was the same orchestra he had led since 1922, eleven years before the Nazis came to power. The only charge was the appointment as Prussian State Councillor, which Furtwängler had tried to resign without success. Furtwängler had not contended that his resignation as Permanent Conductor of the Berlin Philharmonic was a result of arguments with Goebbels over the retention of Jewish musicians: the resignation was the result of the attacks on Paul Hindemith, a non-Jewish composer. Yet as proof of Furtwängler's "deceit," Clark mentions the "former business manager of the Philharmonic who appeared as a defense witness," whose testimony showed other, more selfish reasons for Furtwängler's resignation. The witness was Hans von Benda, a former member of the Nazi party, installed by the Government as "Intendant" or business manager of the Philharmonic when Berta Geissmar was forced out of her position in 1935. He was not a defense witness at all, but a witness for the prosecution, summoned by the court—in spite of his own Nazi background—to present support for its case. His testimony, as Furtwängler showed, offered no details as to the "pressure of guest engagements outside Germany": in the three years following his resignation and reappearance in German musical life, Furtwängler had reduced his conducting at home and abroad, and had devoted considerable time to composing. His two *Violin Sonatas* and his *Piano Concerto* date from these years of semi-retirement. Clark omits a significant charge from Benda's testimony: Furtwängler's alleged anti-Semitism. He had made a remark, Benda testified, that "De Sabata the Jew couldn't conduct Brahms." This evoked a dramatic, heated exchange between Furtwängler, the Tribunal and its witness. Furt-wängler denied vehemently ever having made such a remark: not only was he unaware of the fact that de Sabata was Jew-ish, but even if so, this would certainly not affect his musi-cianship. Furthermore, he had invited de Sabata to Berlin to conduct the Philharmonic many times. On further ques-tioning, Benda wavered and maintained that he heard the remark from an adjoining office, through the wall. He de-parted from the stand quite discredited.

The assistance given by Furtwängler to Jewish musicians is admitted by Clark, though he questions Furtwängler's motives. There were several such musicians and members of their families present on the second day of the trial, all testi-fying for Furtwängler. A member of the Tribunal earlier had tried to establish that Furtwängler had intervened only for famous Jewish figures such as Otto Klemperer, Max Rein-hardt, Bruno Walter and Arnold Schoenberg: this contention was refuted by the presence of the Berlin Philharmonic per-sonnel and their families, none of whom was famous. And a particularly specific refutation came from Mark Hendricks Leuschner, a violinist:

"Furtwängler intervened on my behalf before he knew anything about me as an artist. He continued to protect me for four more years. In fact, he gave me unlimited protection. After every rehearsal, and every concert, he was besieged by people in my position. It was very dangerous for him but he helped us in spite of this!"

Leuschner went on to make a full statement expressing the gratitude of all the persecuted in the musical world for Furtwängler's aid. Furtwängler himself observed, "I could do nothing against governmental anti-Semitic policies, but I could help in individual cases." None of the Jewish witnesses was mentioned by name in Clark's article, nor was their testimony treated in detail.

A large portion of the article was devoted to the case of van der Nüll, who "dared" praise Karajan. His name was consistently misspelled. The technique of convenient omission is the same.

"As for the unproved charge, the substance was that Von der Nuell, music critic of the *Berliner Zeitung,* had in 1938 praised Karajan to the skies and suggested that 50-year-old conductors should learn from him. The reference to Furtwängler was inescapable. Because it was so extravagant and spoke of "the wonder Karajan" this review became known to Berlin musical circles as "Die Wunderkritik" and became a cause célèbre.
It was definitely established that Furtwängler appealed to the management of orchestra and state opera to do something to punish Von der Nuell and both refused. Whereupon, as Furtwängler eventually admitted after a day of denials, he personally and in writing appealed to the Propaganda Ministry to restrain Von der Nuell.

Furtwängler contended he so acted because Von der Nuell's criticism was part of a persecution campaign engineered by Herman Goering, who wanted to get rid of him. It was well established that Von der Nuell, no lily himself, was a personal friend of Goering. The trial resolved itself into a debate on two questions: First, did Furtwängler succeed in his efforts to have the critic punished? Second, was his act that of a sensitive temperamental artist who felt insulted, or that of a very powerful man who desired to suppress all opposition, however legitimate?"

It was not "definitely established that Furtwängler appealed to the management of orchestra and state opera to do something to punish Von der Nuell and both refused." Benda testified that Furtwängler had said he felt that certain circles stood behind these reviews; the facts in his testimony on the point ended there. He added, however, "I had the impression that the defendant expected me to see to it that van der Nüll did not write any more." Benda's role as witness for the prosecution has been mentioned; his interpretation of Furtwängler's remark was entirely in character, and in no way "definitely established" that Furtwängler appealed to him to punish van der Nüll. Furtwängler broke in again and denied ever having given such an impression; he had stated his suspicions of governmental support of the campaign by van der Nüll, nothing more. As for the State Opera which, Clark wrote, had also "refused" Furtwängler's appeal for intervention: Heinz Tietjen, the Director of the Berlin State Opera in 1938, testified that van der Nüll told him personally that the aggressive campaign was not entirely his own but was also an assignment from the editorial staff of his newspaper, in accordance with the wishes of the government. Nothing in Tietjen's testimony referred to any appeal by Furtwängler, or to any refusal. Clark's next statement, that Furtwängler "eventually admitted after a day of denials, he personally and in writing appealed to the Propaganda Ministry to restrain Von der Nuell" is misleading; there was no "day of denials." Without advance briefing of the charges he was to face in the trial, Furtwängler had no access to correspondence and could not remember the date of his protest. This date was May 22, 1939, seven months after the intensive campaign against him had begun.

It was not "well established that Von der Nuell, no lily himself, was a personal friend of Goering." It was established by a witness not mentioned in this detailed article, that van der Nüll had connections in Goering's Ministry which he had used. Clark next sets out to prove correct the second of the two questions he raises: ". . . was his act . . . that of a very powerful man who desired to suppress all opposition, however legitimate?" His technique of manipulated evidence is again brought to bear.

"It soon appeared that the only witness who might answer these questions was Von der Nuell himself, but he was listed as a prisoner of war in Belgium, allegedly as a result of Furtwängler having him drafted.

However, one of the last witnesses was a pathetic, plump Hausfrau, wife of Von der Nuell, who had not heard from her husband since the end of the war and did not know whether he was alive or dead. In timid, weary, scarcely audible tones, she said that she had heard of 'Die Wunderkritik,' but since it had been written before her marriage, she did not know details of the case.

No, she couldn't see any connection between Furtwängler's Olympian anger and her husband's being drafted because there was a two-year interval between the two incidents, and meanwhile the *Berliner Zeitung* had ceased publication, depriving Von der Nuell of exemption.

Thus the main part of the case against Furtwängler collapsed because a man, either dead or missing, who himself might have been a denazification defendant, could not be found, and no one else knew facts or would tell.

Toward the end it seemed as though the denazification tribunal accepted the thesis that if Furtwängler was unsuccessful in his efforts to have the critic punished, then he was innocent, and that if Karajan was not as great a conductor as the critic said, then the efforts were not unjustified. It soon became apparent that this tall, bald-headed old man with a fringe of white hair would be acquitted."

"The only witness who might answer these questions was Von der Nuell himself" was not true. He was not listed as a prisoner of war in Belgium, and evidence brought forward proved that there had been no connection between Furtwängler's protest of May 1939 and van der Nüll's later induction into military service. In addition to the testimony of Tietjen as to the source of the anti-Furtwängler campaign, Dr. Julius Kapp, the Press Chief of the Berlin State Opera before the war, testified as to the real motive of the campaign; one Dr. Westphal, a personal friend of van der Nüll, testified that van der Nüll himself had told him that the Goering Ministry was behind the campaign; Werner Fiedler, a prominent Berlin theatre critic, testified that it was no secret in press circles who was prompting van der Nüll's reviews. But the most important and detailed testimony regarding van der Nüll was given by a former colleague on the same newspaper, Frau Annalise Wiener, on the second day of the trial. Frau Wiener had come to report the Denazification proceedings on the first day, and had volunteered evidence on van der Nüll for the second. Her remarks are most interesting, in view of her own personal danger as a "non-Aryan" in the Hitler years of which she spoke.

"Van der Nüll wished, not only to write reviews but to influence musical life, and give direction to it, by his controversial opinions. In the Third Reich this was almost impossible when one was not protected 'from above'; that is, a writer could carry on a polemic for or against a thing only if a high office agreed with such a controversy and, indeed, considered this polemic as its own. Without a doubt, van der Null actually was convinced that the conductor von Karajan earned the passionate assistance he had rendered him. His enthusiasm for von Karajan's performances knew no bounds. Furtwängler he characterized to me again and again as a conductor 'who belonged to the previous generation,' who undoubtedly had done great services, but in his own eyes, must be more or less forced to realize that 'his time had passed,' and that people like Karajan now had their turn to succeed Furtwängler, whom he discarded like a piece of old iron. In this temper van der Null wrote his reviews. The view declared in the so-called 'Wunderkritik,' that '50-year-olds should follow the example of Karajan,' was absolutely directed at Furtwängler; and not only I and others understood it as such, but we felt it also showed a gross lack of taste. Van der Null admitted to my questions without hesitation that he wanted to wound Furtwängler with this sentence. Not only I, but also colleagues and interested circles of the public considered van der Null's method of writing crude, and his attitude rowdy and beyond all bounds of propriety. It made no difference what opinion we ourselves had about the performances of Furtwängler or Karajan. It was above all the tone of Null's polemic which appeared insolent and impertinent. . . . He took a childish pleasure in recounting what good connections he had with the Ministry of Hermann Goering, which he referred to as the 'Hermann Ministry.' How these connections were, and when they began, I do not know. Van der Null frequently told me that this 'fight for Karajan' and 'fight against Furtwängler' were inseparable and were carried on with the support of the circles around Hermann Goering: that is, that he, van der Null, was not only encouraged by these circles, in this fight, but that it was the project of the 'Hermann Ministry' itself that Karajan be played off against Furtwängler.

. . . Only thus can it be understood that van der Nüll was in a position to lead this 'battle.' Because this 'fight' was protected 'from above'—that is, through Goering's Ministry—in fact promoted and incited by it, we can only speak of 'steering' here. Never would it have been possible for any critic to behave in such a way if he did not have the order 'from above' to begin, and was not protected as he went on. Van der Nüll had an insurmountable advantage over other colleagues who did not share his opinion of Furtwängler. He used this advantage in allowing himself to be 'steered' to the utmost degree.

. . . In this situation, it is only too understandable that Furtwängler was obliged to interpret as a personal affront the massive and crude attacks against him which were concomitant with excessive praise of Karajan. As I already pointed out, he was not the only one who thought so, by any means. Further, it is only too understandable that Furtwängler rightly scented the political figures in the background behind van der Nüll and felt his reviews 'steered.' I believe I have shown that Furtwängler suspected correctly. Since Furtwängler rightly scented behind all this the intrigues of a political group, indeed a group which held dictatorial power, one can hardly blame him if he tried to resist it. Only thus can it be understood that Furtwängler was angry and took steps to oppose this campaign. To silence a local critic was far from his mind; having such an international reputation, he did not need to do this. But this was not a question of one critic, but of a campaign of a dictatorial group against him."

Concerning the later career of van der Nüll, Frau Wiener added:

"Van der Nüll served further as first critic of the *BZ*, without experiencing the slightest difficulty, until his age group was inducted. After the conclusion of basic training he did not go to the front but took over the leadership of a Luftwaffe service-center; his work there consisted, as far as I know, in organizing entertainments for troops on active duty. He held this position in Berlin for nearly the entire duration of the war, and applied voluntarily, as far as I am informed, for front-line duty in 1945."

She nominated the Berlin concert agent Körtling, who had found van der Nüll dead after the fighting in Potsdam, to testify presently; the Tribunal, however, after Frau Wiener's thorough discussion of all points, ruled that Körtling's appearance was unnecessary. The prosecution's case on the van der Nüll affair was at an end. It will be recalled that Clark had written:

> "Thus a main part of the case against Furtwängler collapsed, because a man, either dead or missing, who himself might have been a denazification defendant, could not be found, and no one else knew facts or would tell."

His final "interpretation" of this aspect of the trial is erroneous: nothing had been said as to whether Furtwängler was unsuccessful or not, or whether Karajan was so great or not. These topics would not have altered in the least the character of the press campaign against Furtwängler or his justifiable reaction to it. The part of the case concerning van der Nüll collapsed because of the testimony of Tietjen, Kapp, Westphal, Fiedler, Frau Wiener above all, and Frau van der Nüll: only the latter was mentioned by Clark.[6] His final paragraphs continue in the same vein:

---

[6] On conditions in the German press during the Nazi period, Frau Wiener added in her testimony: "Every initiated person—critic, journalist, artist—knew that we 'observers' in the Third Reich were not permitted simply to praise, but that we were given to understand, from case to case, how emphatically or weakly we should praise. Almost daily a telephone call came from the Propaganda Ministry or from some other office, and the head critic

"On strict rules of evidence of a United States Court it is more than probable he would have been acquitted. Yet throughout the case his attitude was scarcely that of an opponent of nazism despite his statements for the record. He consistently referred to Hitler as 'Der Führer' and used the official Nazi epithet in references to the Weimar Republic. The very term, Weimar Republic, was banned by Hitler with the word 'Systemzeit,' substituted, and this was the word Furtwängler used until one member of the court sharply interjected: 'Would you mind stop using this Nazi expression? It is something we all want to forget.'

Furtwängler replied, 'Oh, was that a Nazi phrase? I was unaware of it.'

The next time, in heavily accented, almost sarcastic tones, he used the words 'Weimar Republic,' whereupon the audience that packed the courtroom seemed vastly amused.

Another member of the court angrily asked the reason for mirth saying, 'What is the reason for this silly laughter? The audience appears to be still somewhat spoiled.' "

Frau Wiener has studied Clark's article and has provided a dossier of corrections, some of which have been noted here. Regarding the use of the word "Systemzeit" she wrote that

---

was told how the review about one artist or another was to be handled. This or that artist 'was not at the moment acceptable' and for his reason should be treated indifferently; others were 'especially worthy of advancement' and should be extolled. One can easily realize what tightrope-walking we critics had to perform in order to say what we felt was right in spite of all this 'steering.' It is well known that we developed the art of writing between the lines and of phrasing our opinions of performances in such a way that the reader could see at once how the event really had been. Extravagant praise, I wish to emphasize, was only possible if a high office especially sanctioned or directly demanded it." For recent studies of the topic see Oron J. Hale, *The Captive Press in the Third Reich* (Princeton, Princeton University Press, 1964) and Ernest K. Bramsted, *Goebbels and National Socialist Propaganda* 1925-1945 (East Lansing, Michigan State University Press, 1965), esp. pp. 88 ff.

"the word is considerably older than the Nazi era. I can remember very well hearing this word spoken by older people in the years after the First World War. In fact, no one would have thought of it when he used it, it was so popular and automatic." The word "Führer," employed in Nazi Germany and abroad for twelve years, came to be similarly automatic. The American press used the word throughout the Nazi period, and virtually all Western historians have done so as well. Frau Wiener added that "the place where the public laughed was entirely different. I laughed out loud myself, when Tribunal Member Schmidt asked his idiotic question, whether Furtwängler believed that Jews couldn't conduct Brahms! I was nearly ejected from the room when the chairman's remark was made."[7]

Clark then concluded:

"Character witnesses produced much testimony of Furtwängler's refusal to act in a propaganda film. One critic, Werner Fiedler, wrote an unfavorable review of the film in question in which Richard Strauss substituted for Furtwängler, and immediately, he testified, he was called in by the conductor for a discussion of the necessity of criticism in general. However, he said Furtwängler finally agreed that criticism is necessary if art is to survive.

At the trial's close Furtwängler rose, tall, slender, self-confident and with the air of a Gothic Jesus, and addressed his admirers in the court room: 'I don't regret having done this for Germans and for Germany. I knew it was worth while to take it.'

This curtain speech brought enthusiastic applause

[7] Herr Schmidt did not forget Frau Wiener's ridicule. As she learned much later, he had then tried to prevent her receiving a license to broadcast on the North West German Radio. The license was obtained for her through the efforts of Rudolf Pechel, a former leader in the German Resistance Movement, who had considerable influence with the British authorities in charge of the network.

which he acknowledged with several bows as in the old days.

He has gone to Switzerland to await review by the Allied Kommandatura of the decision in his case. Earlier, he said his one desire was to clear his name, not conduct, but now associates say he meant he did not want to be permanent conductor of the Philharmonic, just to have ten or so guest appearances a year."

The film in question was a falsified history of the Berlin Philharmonic, made under the special patronage of Goebbels. Furtwängler had refused to appear in it, and the best Goebbels could do was to have a scene filmed in the Artists' Room of the *Philharmonie* showing Furtwängler's portrait on the wall. Werner Fiedler, who had already once been under ban, and a second time had been given a warning by the Propaganda Ministry, gave the long-awaited and much-publicized film a scathing review, "Symphony and Love," so scathing that the director of the film, Paul Verhoeven, demanded that Fiedler be arrested, as Fiedler later learned from American personnel who found the protest in Goebbels' files. Furtwängler was so delighted with Fiedler's review of this distasteful film that he asked to see him: the discussion on criticism in the latter days of December 1944 took place when both men were in personal danger. This was clear from evidence presented. Furtwängler fled Germany a few weeks later and the final months of confusion and collapse in Berlin diverted Goebbels' energies from punishing Fiedler's defiance. The closing remarks made by Furtwängler were more extensive than the one sentence reported by Clark, and they were delivered not with arrogance but with the quiet confidence of a victor.

He reviewed briefly several points concerning his resistance to the Nazis, which had already been discussed during the trial, and then continued:

"Art has nothing to do with power politics, with war, with anything that arises from hatred among nations and spreads it. Art stands above these conflicts. There *must* be things which proceed entirely from the union of mankind, things which represent and prove that union. It is doubly necessary to say this today. Religion, science and art serve this function. Certainly art and music bear witness to the nation from which they spring; but they bear witness to its eternal essence, not its daily policies. Though art proceeds from nations, it stands entirely above them. It is the political function of art, especially in our time, to be above politics.

When I remained in Germany as an unpolitical artist above politics, by that very fact I had already opposed a régime which had degraded art into an instrument of politics. I knew that Germany was in a terrible crisis; I felt responsible for German music, and it was my task to help it survive this crisis, as much as I could. The concern that my art was being misused for propaganda purposes had to yield to the greater concern that German music be preserved, that music be given to the German public by its own musicians. These people, the compatriots of Bach and Beethoven, of Mozart and Schubert, still had to go on living under the control of a régime obsessed with total war. No one who did not live here himself in those days can possibly judge what it was like. Does Thomas Mann really believe that in 'the Germany of Himmler' one should not be permitted to play Beethoven? Could he not realize, that people never needed more, never yearned more to hear Beethoven and his message of freedom and human love, than precisely these Germans, who had to live under the Himmler terror? I do not regret having stayed with them."

The applause was warm and enthusiastic. It did not come only from Furtwängler's "admirers." The room was small, filled with German and foreign correspondents, Allied officers, witnesses and their families. The applause was general.

Considerable attention has been given to correcting misstatements in Delbert Clark's article, and some points omitted entirely have now been noted. But the list of errors is not yet complete. There are other serious omissions of evidence.

Perhaps the deepest impression at the trial was made by Clemens Herzberg, the Jewish business manager for Max Reinhardt for many years before the war and in 1946 Director of the State Opera in the Russian Sector of Berlin. Herzberg, who had himself suffered persecution and had lived in hiding during the Nazi years, appeared as a character witness for Furtwängler on the second day. He testified that he had known Furtwängler for nearly forty years, and he made a special point that Furtwängler had remained loyal to his Jewish friends throughout the régime when many Germans did not dare to do so. He recalled a meeting with Reinhardt in Paris in 1933, after the publication of Furtwängler's Open Letter to Goebbels. Reinhardt had said, "I hope that Furtwängler stays in Germany. People like him *must* stay there if Germany is to survive. I would have stayed myself, if I had been allowed. Tell that to Furtwängler when you see him!" A letter from Reinhardt in 1934 was read, expressing a similar reaction over the Hindemith case.

Boleslav Barlog, a film director, gave testimony of numerous incidents when Furtwängler had criticized the régime in public, at a time when Germans were being beheaded daily for expressing "defeatist" sentiments.[8] Franz Jastrau, the

---

[8] For a good description of the tense atmosphere with Security Service (S.D.) informers at work everywhere in Nazi Germany after 1938, see William L. Shirer, *The Rise and Fall of the Third Reich, A History of Nazi Germany* (New York, Simon and Schuster, Inc., 1960), p. 273: "Under the expert hand of Heydrich . . . the S.D. soon spread its net over the country, employing some 100,000 part-time informers who were directed to snoop on every citizen in the land and report the slightest remark or activity which was deemed inimical to Nazi rule. No one—if he were not foolish—said or did anything that might be interpreted as "anti-Nazi" without first taking precautions that it was not being recorded by hidden S.D. microphones or overheard

attendant of the Philharmonic for many years, related incidents when Furtwängler had insulted the Nazis by refusing to give the German salute before concerts, though many around him felt he was thus endangering the Orchestra and begged him to do so. The members of the Berlin Philharmonic and their wives, whom Furtwängler had shielded, gave accounts of their individual cases. Furtwängler himself gave accounts of his refusals, in over sixty cases, to conduct at concerts of a political nature in spite of constant pressure from the government; each refusal had to be accompanied by a medical certificate and detailed reports from his physician. Similar pressures were exerted on him to lead tours in the occupied countries; he had refused. Most important of all, he and his secretary Agathe von Thiedemann recounted the story of his escape from Nazi Austria in early 1945.

Fräulein Dr. Richter, a physician treating Frau Himmler, had been told of conversations overheard by household servants, to the effect that Furtwängler was suspected of complicity in the July 20, 1944 plot against Hitler, several of whose members were his friends. He was being placed under Nazi ban and would henceforth be watched constantly. Dr. Richter appeared suddenly at five o'clock in the morning at his Potsdam home in November 1944, in order to inform him of this. Two months later she came again on another secret visit, reporting that her sources had overheard that Furtwängler was to be "eliminated" in a matter of days. Furtwängler went to Vienna immediately and while ostensibly preparing a concert, he explained his difficult position to the Swiss Consul. He was given a visa, and after his concert he disappeared from Vienna. Gestapo officers arrested

---

by an S.D. agent. Your son or your father or your wife or your cousin or your best friend or your boss or your secretary might be an informer for Heydrich's organization; you never knew, and if you were wise nothing was ever taken for granted."

his secretary and interrogated her; but she had not been told where he was going, and could not be of use to them. When the German Foreign Office learned that Furtwängler was in Switzerland a few days later, it demanded his extradition at once. The Swiss, however, granted him political asylum.[9]

These are some of the details omitted in Delbert Clark's account of the Denazification proceedings. Its length suggested a full treatment of what had transpired; but its intention was obviously not to inform objectively.[10] Furtwängler was shocked at this article; but he did not send a protest to the *Times* or demand that it print his refutation. Instead he sent a dossier of corrections to his friend Carleton Smith in America, asking him to publish it.

> "I was astonished to see that though the trial had cleared every single detail in my favor, the *New York Times* brought an account of it which was forged in large parts, and that the accounts in the American-controlled press in Germany were not objective either. This is one of the reasons why it is absolutely necessary that the public should be informed of the facts about me."

This was an ineffective method of rebuttal. Yet it is entirely possible that the *Times* would not have carried his refutation. A short time later, Professor Victor Zuckerkandl,[11] whose

[9] Gilbert Back, formerly of the Berlin Philharmonic, wrote that "I learned from a member of the Swiss Embassy in Ankara in early 1945 that the Swiss Government had given orders to all border posts to let Furtwängler into the country, whether he tried to cross the frontier by train, automobile, on foot, or even on skis." Cf. *Furtwängler Recalled*, p. 92.

[10] For a very brief but essentially unchanged view of the trial, see Clark's *Again the Goose Step, the Lost Fruits of Victory* (New York, The Bobbs-Merrill Company, Inc., 1949), p. 223.

[11] Later author of *Sound and Symbol: Music and the External World* (Princeton, Princeton University Press, 1956), and *The Sense of Music* (Princeton, Princeton University Press, 1959).

life Furtwängler had saved before the war, wrote him from America that the *Times* had failed to publish his letter-to-the-editor defending Furtwängler.

Other things were on Smith's mind. He felt that all political difficulties would disappear once Furtwängler began conducting in America, and with this in view, he offered him the Directorship of the Aspen, Colorado Festival, then being organized. The industrialists who were planning the Festival were eager to have him. On April 11, 1947, Smith wrote.

> "Great admirers of yours, they are willing to give you a three-year contract, arrange a house for you and your family there, and make it possible for you to assemble and rehearse a Furtwängler Orchestra with which you can record, broadcast, and tour the country."

Furtwängler was moved by this offer, but he maintained that a rehabilitation must come before he began conducting in America. He regretted that he was not thirty years younger to participate in the organization and development of such a new Festival. He had difficulties to face at home, moreover, before he could think of taking on a new post in America. The Allied ratification of the Denazification acquittal had been promised "soon," but months were slipping by and no action was being taken. On March 4, 1947, Furtwängler had written Smith:

> "As I hear from a very well informed source, the expected ratification of my case by the Allies is to be postponed for a long time, maybe for years. The responsible authorities at Berlin spoke openly about this, saying that it 'had to be prevented on all accounts that I could come to America within the coming years'."

A few days earlier, in relating this information to Fritz Zweig in Los Angeles, Furtwängler had added:

"I have known for a long time that such considerations are playing a role. But should this be a reason that Berlin and Germany must wait, that I cannot conduct elsewhere abroad? I am ready and willing to declare that I do not intend to go to America in the near future, if something could be gained for Europe by this . . ."

And on March 19, he wrote Zweig:

"New light has just been thrown on the Allied procrastination by a notice in the Swiss press that 'new material' has been found, and has been given to the Denazification commission which handled my case for decision as to opening the trial anew . . ."

Zweig replied a week later that Friedelinde Wagner had sent the State Department ten written affidavits by émigrés in America whom Furtwängler had helped during the Nazi years, in order to serve as defense material if the case should be reopened. As events turned out, it never was. Furtwängler had forced the Allies' hand by accepting invitations for concerts in Italy, beginning April 6. He sent word of this to Berlin, and since the Allied Kommandatura had no jurisdiction over Italy and could not prevent his appearances there, it ratified the acquittal on April 27, allowing him to conduct in all occupied zones as well.

For the first time in over two years, Furtwängler led an orchestra again, and began his second career. There were difficulties. On May 9, 1947, he wrote Smith:

". . . The Allied declaration about my Denazification, which was published here saying that the Allies had confirmed the German verdict that acquitted me of Nazi collaboration, is only partly or not published at all in other countries. Invitations to Milan, Salzburg, etc. are called off and 'forbidden' at the last moment under influences from America. The political misrepresentations go on as before though the material about me proved that they were ill-founded. What am I to do about this state of affairs? I wait for someone to stand up for me who dares to call things by their names. This must and can only be done in America."

Five days later he wrote Zweig:

". . . In Italy I was still to conduct one more concert, in Milan, which was cancelled at the last moment after a telephone protest from Toscanini. I was dismissed and Issay Dobrowen was engaged to replace me."

This was indeed ironic, since Dobrowen owed his escape from Nazi Germany to Furtwängler alone.

A little more than a week later, Furtwängler gave his first concert with the Berlin Philharmonic since January 1945, sponsored by the United States Military Government. Berliners stood in lines all night waiting for the box-office to open, and when the concert was sold out, some tried to barter for tickets with cigarettes, coffee, chinaware, oil paintings, clothing, or whatever they had. Allied officers and soldiers, the press corps, prominent figures in Berlin social and cultural life were in the audience at the *Titania Palast*, and hundreds of the public Furtwängler had stayed in Nazi Germany to serve. His program was the *Egmont Overture*, the *Pastorale* and *Fifth Symphonies* of Beethoven, recalling the previous reappearance before his Berlin audience in April 1935. The atmosphere was as electric as it had been on that night twelve years earlier. When Furtwängler appeared on the stage, his Orchestra rose and the audience thundered its welcome. Furtwängler raised his hand for silence and began the *Egmont*. When the concert had ended, the audience again broke into wild applause. John Elliot of the *New York Herald Tribune* reported the enthusiastic reception given Furtwängler and soon found his article under attack by Erika Mann, daughter of Thomas Mann, who wired to the *Herald Tribune:*

"In a Berlin dispatch datelined May 25, Mr. John Elliot describes the 'tumultuous acclaim' given to Dr. Wilhelm Furtwängler, recently 'denazified' German conductor, when he led the Berlin Philharmonic Orchestra for the first time since the war. 'A cosmopolitan crowd,' says Mr. Elliot, 'forgot nationality and the aftermemories of the war.' And then he quotes Mr. Erich Clarke, chief of the Theatre, Film and Music Branch of the Information Control Division of the American Military Government, as follows: 'I was glad to see people forget all about politics for once and lose themselves in music . . .' 'The crowd applauded for fifteen minutes forcing the conductor to return sixteen times to the platform to acknowledge the cheers of his admirers.'

Who were these 'admirers' and what caused them to applaud for fifteen minutes? According to Mr. Elliot an international audience paid tribute to a conductor for the good and simple reason that they liked his music. And no doubt, Dr. Furtwängler knows his stuff even when—as was the case on the evening in question—he has had only one or two rehearsals and the orchestra, a makeshift ensemble two-thirds of whose members were not with him when the maestro last conducted the Philharmonic early in 1945, is not up to standards. Let us assume, then, that the concert was good. Owing to some minor miracle, it may even have been excellent.

But excellent concerts are being given continually in New York, Boston and Philadelphia, without prompting American music lovers to applaud for fifteen minutes. Nor do I remember any concert in Paris or London the acclaimed excellence of which forced the audience to force the conductor to return sixteen times to the platform. As for Moscow, I do not know, but it appears unlikely that the Soviets should have 'forgotten nationality and the aftermemories of the war' in honor of a personage whom, along with their Allies, they prevented from appearing for almost two years.

It would seem, then, that Dr. Furtwängler owes his triumph chiefly to his compatriots. Had these, however, really 'forgotten all about politics and lost themselves in music?' Or were they not rather using or abusing music for the purpose of staging a political demonstration?

Much speaks in favor of the latter assumption. 'Denazification,' as is generally known, is most unpopular with the Germans who will miss no opportunity noisily, pointedly and aggressively to celebrate its 'victims' and 'survivors.' They have done so—to cite one example where many could be given—in the case of Gustav Gruendgens, actor, director, Nazi 'Staatsrat,' Senator and intimate friend of Goering, when the Russians finally persuaded his reappearance on a Berlin stage. They have done so in the case of Dr. Furtwängler, Hitler's pet maestro and musical propagandist abroad. And they will continue to do so as long as Allied reporters keep mistaking their strictly political demonstrations for art-loving ovations.

That a number (just how large a number one would like to know) of non-Germans contributed to Furtwängler's conquest of Berlin hardly alters the character of the German performance. This character is further illustrated by the fact that no great anti-Fascist conductor or virtuoso has thus far been urged to stage a comeback in Berlin. Neither Toscanini nor Bruno Walter, neither Huberman nor Adolf Busch, men of whose world-renowned art 'Führer' Hitler deprived his musical nation, seems to be wanted.

Zürich, May 31, 1947"

This cable led indirectly to a remarkable correspondence between Furtwängler and Thomas Mann. It began for quite different reasons, but the discussion mainly treated political problems. Mann had been recently invited by an association of German writers to come and live in Germany, where he might learn from colleagues what conditions had been like under Hitler. The implication that he was poorly informed

91

enraged him and to some extent accounted for the tone of his letter to Furtwängler.

On June 29, 1947, Furtwängler wrote from Clarens:

"I have just come from Munich, where I met Frau Heinz Pringsheim briefly. She and her husband are still having difficulties with their departure for Switzerland. Frau Pringsheim thought that the best thing would be for your daughter Erika, as an American citizen, to come to pick them up in Munich with her car. Frau Pringsheim asked me to send this request along to you.

Quite a while ago I had written a reply to one of your publications on 'Germany and the Germans,' but subsequently did not carry out my intention to send it to you. However, I would now welcome the opportunity of talking over German problems with you, if this be convenient, wherein my own, finally settled case would play only the slightest role. In view of the attitude of those around you towards me, I do not know how you feel about such a suggestion, and naturally do not wish to have my proposal refused. Nor do I know how long you will remain in Switzerland. In case you do not answer these lines, I shall assume you prefer that we do not see each other."

On July 1, Mann sent his reply:

"I should consider it improper to leave unanswered the handwritten letter of the man in whom I see the greatest conductor of our time—as you suggest, this would imply a rejection of your proposal. We should not even discuss a rejection. But an exchange of ideas on Germany which would indeed include your own case, for me not 'settled' at all, would really have little sense and offer slight prospect of agreement. I approve of your written defense, which Alma Mahler-Werfel gave me to read, as little as I approve of the fifteen-minute demonstration in Berlin, which you allowed by returning to the platform sixteen times. I know the present-day moods and conditions in Germany better than those who have stayed behind, who impose silence on me, but still want me to come there, in order that I be 'tactfully advised' (this was the phrase used). And as for the past, 'Germany and the Germans' was an attempt to explain to a well-meaning American public how everything in Germany could develop as it has. I take it that you have written a polemic against this—what might be false in it—though I am inclined to believe that your real displeasure was caused more by the truth in it. In general, we are not a very truthful people and we hate psychology because our own is all too strange.

There are still difficulties for our relatives to come here. However, we were able to greet my younger brother at the border, in fact to drive him to Zürich for a day's visit."

Three days later Furtwängler wrote back:

"I thank you for the letter which I could receive from you. You are very frank in it; please allow me to be frank as well.

First, my own 'case,' about which I really did not wish to speak, which is still, as you write, not at all 'settled' for you. Should you, the great psychologist, who know the nature of the public from your own experience, not know that the 'Furtwängler case' for all those informed—and that is a rather large German public— was never for a moment a real case to be heard by a Denazification Tribunal at all? In Germany everyone knew and knows that from the beginning I resisted more than any other musician, with all the influence I could bring to bear, in great as in small incidents, without prejudice to the fact that I was exhibited and photographed for Hitler's propaganda. With the aid of a section of the American press, the story has been grossly exaggerated or invented by shameless lies which have continued until the most recent reports of the trial (cf. *New York Times*), lies against which I have no weapons.

Now, you say you have read my written defense and disapprove of it. May I ask, of what exactly do you disapprove in it? The decision of the three Austrian and German Commissions which acquitted me one after the other? The fact that I considered it right to stay in Germany—a view I still hold today?

I certainly do not claim that I have always acted correctly in my life. But my written defense is addressed to a German Denazification court. And I know quite as well as any of those who today sit on Tribunals in Germany, what struggle against Nazism means.

I do not understand you clearly enough here, so I shall turn to another clearer point. You reproach me for having caused a fifteen-minute ovation instead of making music.

First: this concert was thoroughly prepared by many more than 'one or two rehearsals.' The orchestra is today, except for a small fraction, the old Berlin Philharmonic Orchestra. When a real demonstration was about to begin—at the *first* appearance before the public in two years—I did not allow it, but began immediately with the music. My retention at the end of the concert, however, was the natural and understandable result of expressions of friendly applause, nothing more.

Nevertheless, should you and your daughter Erika have entirely forgotten what music means to the Germans and always has meant to them? When I had finished a performance of *Tristan* in Vienna in 1943, the ovation for the singers at the close of this five-hour work lasted thirty-two minutes—as it was timed—and at last had to be ended by myself.

Fifteen-minute ovations are nothing unusual for Berlin—and Beethoven. I enclose a letter I received today, wherein a musician writes of my recent concert in Hamburg, after which the same thing occurred. You must bear in mind that Beethoven and Brahms are things which one cannot steal from the Germans even today— thank God such things still exist—and things in which they can find themselves in the true and grand sense, far from Hitler and his seduction. Do you, the great psychologist, the great German writer, begrudge them this rediscovery, disparage and discriminate against it?

As for myself, relatively unimportant in this general connection, do you feel that the people should not also have a little right to be happy when someone who has been slandered by lying maneuvers and dishonestly kept from them for two years, finally returns? All of this does not have the slightest thing to do with politics.

I believed—as I wrote to you, without finally sending the message—that in your case I had to distinguish between statements that were born of momentary emotions and those that concern essentials. If you said somewhere that Beethoven's *Fidelio* should not ring out in 'the Germany of Himmler,' surely you do not maintain this view today. For a 'Germany of Himmler' has never existed, only a Germany raped by Himmler. It would be utterly senseless to insist that in such a country a work that is so German should not ring out. When did any other nation provide the inner potentialities for this work? Your attempt to explain the Germans psychologically to the American public is something else again. Precisely because I believed I feel as you do about the Germans in this respect, and share many of your views, I thought that a personal meeting would be fruitful. For you today the possibilities, and to a certain extent the obligation, to help Germany are very great—regardless of what the Germans themselves might think.

And if I personally must gather from your letter that the breach between us now is still too great, I shall not give up the hope that one day this will change."

There was no reply to this letter, nor any reconciliation.[12] Some months later, when his London audience gave Furt-

---

[12] The Berlin Philharmonic reports that ninety percent of the wartime members of the Orchestra were still in it after the War. The Beethoven *Fifth Symphony* as recorded during this concert in Berlin on May 25, 1947, has been published by Heliodor on S-25078 and is a further refutation of Miss Mann's remarks on the quality of the Orchestra at that time. The sound of the wartime Berlin Philharmonic in Furtwangler's recording of the same work, first issued by the State Recording Company of the Soviet Union on Melodiya D 05800-1 and soon available here on Turnabout TV 4361, is the same.

wängler a ten-minute ovation, and Parisians demonstrated for him during intermission and for a half-hour after his first postwar concert in their city, Thomas Mann and his daughter Erika had nothing to say.

V

IN 1948, Furtwängler was drawn into the most painful episode of his relations with America. On August 10, Dr. Eric Oldberg, Vice-President of the Board of Directors of the Chicago Orchestral Association, wired him that he was being seriously considered for the post of General Music Director of the Chicago Symphony Orchestra. Furtwängler did not reply, and Dr. Oldberg wired again on August 13 requesting an answer. On August 20, Furtwängler wrote:

> "As my secretary told your representative on the telephone, I received your cable of the tenth together with the follow-up cable only a few days ago. I did not answer at once as the decision whether I could come to Chicago, season 1949-50, does not wholly depend on me. I have as a matter of fact negotiations about this season going on with some important music institutions, e.g. Scala/Milan, which I cannot call off at a day's notice. Besides, I cannot omit to say that the calumnies and difficulties of political nature which have kept me away from the States for over ten years have not ceased until now, as far as I am told. I cannot give you a binding confirmation whether I shall be free at that time and therefore believe it would be better for the moment if you did not come over personally. . . ."

Dr. Oldberg replied on August 25:

> ". . . As to your questions about your reception by our American audiences, I assure you that we investigated this thoroughly before communicating with you in the first place. There is no ground for apprehension, whatever, from any group. I can explain this better to you in person than by letter, but you may be absolutely certain that this is the fact, and that it has already been directly ascertained by us without question, from every possible source. I may add that Chicago is particularly fortunate in this respect, though I have no reason to doubt the attitude of any other American city. . . ."

The Chicago Trustees wanted Furtwängler for twenty-two weeks of the twenty-eight week season; Furtwängler wrote on September 4 that he was honored by the confidence the Board of Trustees placed in him with such an offer, but pointed out that a Music Director of an orchestra should spend most of his season with his group. This he was not prepared to do: his work in Germany, in Paris, London, Milan, Vienna and also the Festival centers of Florence, Salzburg, Lucerne and Edinburgh, would have to be curtailed severely by such a commitment in Chicago. He asked that he be allowed to postpone his final decision until he returned from the Edinburgh Festival. That decision came in a letter of September 16. Furtwängler repeated the considerations of prior commitments in Europe, which did not leave enough time for Chicago. The possibility of political repercussions further complicated the situation; his coming as a Guest Conductor for a short visit would not solve the Chicago Orchestra's problem of securing a Music Director; in view of this, he had decided not to accept the offer. A personal meeting, he added, would in no way affect his decision, and he advised against one. Dr. Oldberg was not discouraged by this letter; he wired Furtwängler on September 23 to defer a final answer until he had received another letter. In this letter, dated September 23, Dr. Oldberg emphasized the speed of air travel making international commitments feasible, and mentioned a reduction of the Chicago season to eighteen weeks. He added that no decision as to permanency of the post as Director needed to be made; a year-to-year basis was acceptable to the Board. Shortly thereafter, on October 11, another negotiator for the Chicago Board, George A. Kuyper, wired that he would come to meet Furtwängler in Hamburg on October 18. The meeting was cordial and friendly, but led to no reversal of Furtwängler's decision. On November 1, Edward L. Ryerson, the President of the Chicago Board, wrote Furtwängler that

> ". . . we were all delighted to have Mr. Kuyper's report concerning his discussions with you and to know of the many courtesies you extended to him. He made a full report of his conversations to our Board of Directors, and it was received with the hope that you will reach a favorable conclusion and accept the proposal that was made to you by Mr. Kuyper. I know I express the feelings of every member of the Board in saying that such an answer would be received with the greatest possible enthusiasm not only by the Board but by all of the music lovers in Chicago. . . ."

In early November, a report appeared in the *Chicago Tribune*, sent by its London correspondent, that negotiations to engage Furtwängler were in progress: Kuyper wrote of this to Furtwängler on November 10:

> "Of interest to me is that this report in the paper has produced no repercussions, so I am more than ever certain that the political campaign—about which you expressed some fears—will *never* develop. It was good to talk with you and I trust that I shall see you soon."

99

On November 26, from Paris, Furtwängler answered both men that he had decided against the offer. He regretted that Kuyper's trip had been in vain, and thanked them for their confidence and personal interest in the negotiations.

The Chicago Board did not acknowledge defeat. On December 4, Dr. Oldberg cabled that it hoped Furtwängler would give as many weeks as possible to the Orchestra, and that the question of permanent leadership could be postponed. That same day, some hours later, Kuyper cabled suggestion of a fourteen-week Chicago season; on December 14, Ryerson accepted Furtwängler's terms for an eight-week period at his convenience. The next day, Furtwängler outlined to Mr. Ryerson details of rehearsal time, engagement of colleagues and soloists, and formation of programs. He added a note of warning before closing:

> "I have been afraid that there will be public attacks against me and against yourselves, from certain quarters. What are you planning to do against them? I am not afraid of them, but I do deem it wise if we understand each other promptly concerning action to take in such cases. Attacks of a political nature against me are unfounded on fact, and as soon as I hear of them, I can easily refute them. I must only know how and where they appear.
>
> Finally, may I express my sincere satisfaction that you have successfully concluded these negotiations, somewhat complicated by circumstances and distance. I hope that my work in Chicago will be gratifying and beneficial to all of us."

So ended the negotiations to bring Furtwängler to Chicago in the 1949-50 season. The next letter from Chicago, unsigned, read as follows.

> "Your appearance in the United States and particularly in Chicago is emphatically unwelcome. The cli-

mate in Chicago—a very famous city—would surely be intolerable for your health and would lead to fatal injury—against which Ryerson, Kuyper, Aaron etc. probably cannot give you guaranteed protection.

Consider this warning carefully. It is the only one."

A telegram from one Israel Stern arrived in Vienna: "Big surprises from the Jews of Chicago await you." Furtwängler wrote on December 26, asking Ryerson for his plans against political attacks and for the reaction of the American public to his appointment. He mentioned that he had received warnings already. The answer, a cable from Kuyper on December 28, was quite different from what he had hoped to receive:

"We are informed today that three outstanding conductors whom we had invited to appear as guests and six leading soloists we had planned to engage will refuse to perform with the Chicago Symphony Orchestra if you appear as guest conductor for next season. Surprise to us. Our Trustees feel this presents grave question for our mutual consideration, whether it is wise for you or us to carry out plans for your engagement. Please treat this as strictly confidential and make no statement. Will call you Wednesday."

Furtwängler wired back the next day:

"Silent withdrawal on my part would be synonymous with confession of guilt before the whole public. Therefore withdrawal impossible for me if not first given sufficient opportunity to vindicate myself."

He cabled to Ansermet, then visiting in New York, on the same day:

"Dear Friend: I ask you for help and advice. Try to influence Chicago to give me the opportunity of de-

101

fending myself personally in America, before immeas-
urable harm is done by a final refusal."

and on January 4, cabled Ryerson to publicize the fact that
American musicians such as Bruno Walter and Menuhin had
not protested against his coming. In New York, Howard
Taubman published an article in the *Times* on January 6,
"Musicians' Ban on Furtwängler Ends His Chicago Contract
for '49"; Furtwängler cabled Kuyper on January 8 to wire
him that this reported cancellation was not true. Taubman's
title was somewhat premature, in view of the prolongation
of the affair until January 19, but the article is worth careful
study:

> "A group of world-famous soloists and conductors,
> including Vladimir Horowitz, Artur Rubinstein, and
> Alexander Brailowsky, pianists; Lily Pons, Metropolitan
> Opera soprano; and André Kostelanetz, conductor, have
> warned the Chicago Symphony Orchestra that they
> would not appear as soloists or guest leaders with that
> ensemble if Wilhelm Furtwängler became principal con-
> ductor, it was learned today.
> The board of the Chicago Orchestral Association, as
> a result, has decided not to have Mr. Furtwängler con-
> duct there next season, it was learned. Edward Ryerson,
> president of the association, admitted last month that
> his organization had invited the German conductor to
> Chicago. Since then Chicagoans have made no official
> statement, but Mr. Furtwängler announced in Vienna
> that he had accepted the offer.
> The action taken by leading musicians here on Mr.
> Furtwängler was based on the conductor's war record.
> They maintained that he had remained in Germany
> throughout the war and had conducted leading German
> musical organizations, occasionally in the presence of
> Adolf Hitler and his top aides.
> The protest of American musicians was aimed also
> at Walter Gieseking, German pianist, who is due to

return to this country this month after an absence of about ten years. The objections to Mr. Gieseking were generally the same as those to Mr. Furtwängler.

Mr. Horowitz has warned local concert managers that he would not appear on any series of recitals that also engages Mr. Gieseking. Mr. Rubinstein has taken similar action. This season he declined to appear with the National Symphony Orchestra of Washington which had also engaged Mr. Gieseking.

Mr. Horowitz said that he made his decision about Mr. Furtwängler and Mr. Gieseking out of respect for the hundreds of thousands of Americans who died in the war against nazism. He said that Mr. Furtwängler's international prestige was such that he could have had a career anywhere outside of Germany and that he had ample opportunity to desert nazism.

Mr. Horowitz added that he was prepared to forgive the small fry who had no alternative but to remain and work in Germany. Mr. Furtwängler, however, he said, was out of the country on several occasions and could have elected to keep out.

Mr. Rubinstein sent the following telegram from his home in Beverly Hills, California: 'I will not collaborate, musically or otherwise, with any one who collaborated with Hitler, Goering, and Goebbels. Had Furtwängler been firm in his democratic convictions he would have left Germany. Many persons like Thomas Mann departed from that country in protest against the barbarism of the Nazis. Mr. Furtwängler chose to stay and chose to perform, believing he would be on the side of the victors. Walter Gieseking acted similarly. There are reports that Furtwängler saved some persons from the Nazi régime. This is unconfirmed. Now he wants to earn American dollars and American prestige. He does not merit either.'

It was learned that a number of leading conductors who had been approached to be guest directors in Chicago had declined, if Mr. Furtwängler came. These men refused to have their names used, since they did not wish as conductors to seem to be threatening another conductor, but they did not deny that they had taken such action.

Among other soloists who have taken similar action, it was learned, were Gregor Piatigorsky, 'cellist, and Nathan Milstein and Isaac Stern, violinists. It appeared that these soloists and conductors made their decisions independently and conveyed them to their respective managers for communication to Chicago.

From sources in Chicago it was learned that Mr. Furtwängler had been requested to withdraw. He, in turn, maintained, it was said, that he had a binding contract and expected the Chicago Orchestra to pay him off.

There were other indications that Chicago had decided to forego Mr. Furtwängler's services. When the German conductor announced his engagement some weeks ago he said it would be for the opening of the season. It was learned yesterday that Victor de Sabata, Italian conductor, has been engaged for the first four weeks of the season.

Among other conductors who have agreed to conduct in Chicago next season are Rafael Kubelik, Czech; Fritz Reiner and Fritz Busch. Some of these, it is understood, would not have accepted any engagement if Mr. Furtwängler had been named musical director of the Chicago Orchestra.

Mr. Furtwängler's record has not been without defenders. Yehudi Menuhin, violinist, appeared as soloist with him in Germany about a year ago. Mr. Menuhin said that the conductor had saved the lives of Jewish musicians during the Nazi régime.

Mr. Furtwängler, who has been conducting in Europe since the end of the war, was cleared by a German denazification court. It was held at that time that though he had shown bad judgment and was morally culpable he was not legally guilty.

Mr. Gieseking remained in Germany throughout the war. At first he was barred by the Allied military officials from resuming his career on ground of implication with the Nazis, but later that decision was reversed. He, too, has been playing in public in many European countries."

There are nearly as many errors in this article as in that of Delbert Clark in 1946. Refutation of many emerges from the documents yet to be examined; but the use of phrases such as "it was learned," "it appeared," "from sources in Chicago," "it was said," "it is understood," serving to divest the writer of responsibility for the "facts" he was printing, should be noted. Without debating the points whether Furtwängler should have left Germany as Horowitz and Rubinstein maintained, or the naïveté of their objection to Hitler's attendance at Furtwängler's concerts—who in the Third Reich could have prevented this absolute dictator from coming?—it must be noted that Furtwängler had not "expected the Chicago Orchestra to pay him off" as Taubman reported. The Denazification Court did not hold Furtwängler "morally culpable but not legally guilty"; this is an echo of the main point advanced by Delbert Clark in his account of the trial, not the decision of the Court.

Following publication of this artists' protest, Menuhin, in Rome, telegraphed the Chicago Board:

"I shall have to give up the pleasure of playing with the Chicago Symphony Orchestra until this affair has been clarified. . . . Furtwängler showed firm resistance to the Nazis; he kept as many Jews as possible in the Berlin Philharmonic Orchestra, never undertook propaganda tours, was never a member of the Nazi party . . . He has been denazified by those responsible for clarifying his case, and it is not for us to question their judgment."

His reaction to the artists' protest he published at the same time:

"I have never encountered a more brazen attitude than that of three or four of the ringleaders in their frantic and obvious efforts to exclude an illustrious colleague from their happy hunting grounds. I consider their behavior beneath contempt."

Before Furtwängler's January 8 wire to Kuyper, asking for denial of the cancellation-notice, he received a letter from Ryerson, dated December 31, 1948. It gave for the first time a history of the events facing the Board in Chicago for the past month.

". . . We have talked with Mr. Ansermet twice on the telephone since you cabled him in regard to the situation which has arisen and, in reply, he requested that we give you the circumstances which resulted in our cable to you on December 28. We will try to give as clear a picture as possible of what has occurred.

The Chicago papers, in late November and early December, carried several interviews with you about the possibility of your coming to Chicago, although we had given no statement to the press. Up to that time, we had heard nothing of any opposition to your appearance. In general, the publicity in the papers was favorable, but, after those interviews, we began to receive a few letters of protest which, however, did not really alarm us.

Beginning about the middle of December, we received a protest from the Musicians' Chapter of the American Veterans' Committee, a national organization of ex-soldiers. This was followed shortly by four telegrams from Jewish Women's Organizations in Chicago protesting your selection as guest conductor, copies of which are enclosed. Moreover, letters of protest increased and we were told by a visiting artist and a conductor that a strong opposition in musical circles was developing. We tried to verify this but could get no clear facts, and we continued to feel we could meet whatever opposition would arise.

We received your telegram of acceptance on December 25th and immediately sent out contracts to confirm engagements with other conductors who had been under discussion and were told that strong opposition had arisen—that some *definitely would not come* and others probably would refuse. The same information was given us as to soloists. The persons involved included some of the most prominent conductors and soloists in this country who have played with us repeatedly before, and who have been most friendly and helpful to us through many years. This news was a great shock to us and clearly showed that an 'underground' opposition had been developing to a much greater extent than we could have anticipated.

The papers have begun to carry letters from individuals here objecting to your engagement and we have been told that some conductors and soloists have been warned by telephone not to appear with us if you come. It has been indicated to them that if you are a guest conductor here next season, they will be 'black-listed' so as to prevent their appearances elsewhere.

On Thursday night, December 23rd, a number of men appeared outside the hall before the concert began and distributed copies of the document enclosed quoting Toscanini.[1] The Young Progressives of Illinois named are a political group in Chicago with radical associations.

We are confident now that there is a public 'underground' outside of musical circles which is preparing for mass protests and even for disturbances of the peace. As a result of these developments, our entire Board is firmly convinced that if we bring you here to appear next season as a guest conductor, your position in this country will be irreparably damaged. We believe the result would be equally disastrous as far as the Orchestral Association is concerned. We fear that your concerts could be conducted in an orderly manner only under police protection.

We realize that we have a serious responsibility in having urged you to appear here, in the firm belief

---

[1] This statement was essentially the same as that cited on p. 56 above.—ed.

which we expressed to you that there would be no substantial opposition. We deeply regret what has now occurred, and we are anxious to coöperate with you in every way, to protect your reputation and to clear up this difficulty with the least injury to us both. Our Board of Trustees are of the opinion that it is impossible for us to have you appear here as planned, but we will be pleased to receive any suggestions which you make as to the way in which the change of plans should be made public, and we can assure you that no statement will come from us until you have given us your suggestions. You realize that we must act promptly as it is necessary for us to rearrange our plans for the next season in time to make an announcement of our final plans the fifteenth of January.

In closing let me express my own personal appreciation for your distinguished career and my confidence in your judgment to do what is best for all concerned. It is our hope that the time will soon come when the difficulties we are now encountering throughout the world and especially in this country may be corrected to a degree where it will be possible for us to have the opportunity of fulfilling the plans we are now so reluctantly relinquishing."

Ansermet wrote Furtwängler that Charles Munch told him he had received an anonymous phone call asking if he planned to conduct in Chicago. He answered that he intended to conduct only the Boston Symphony, and then asked "Why?" "Never mind, if you're not going to Chicago, I have nothing to say," was the reply. Ansermet pointed out that the Board had already been in a weak position, because its previous dismissal of Arthur Rodzinski had angered the Chicago musical public; that while those who were hostile to Furtwängler's coming were extremely active, the majority of the public was totally indifferent. Among these "neutrals" no one would lift a finger to help him. Ansermet advised that Furtwängler make a statement "at the express request of the trustees of the orchestra" to give up his appearances next season.

But Furtwängler had decided to fight it out. He sent a long letter of counterproposals to the Board on January 6.

"In the course of our earlier correspondence I have often mentioned and warned about the possibility of political difficulties. I understand completely your situation, but you must also understand that I can under no circumstances, without a word of explanation and without the slightest attempt at a public rectification, give up this already concluded engagement. Such a course would mean that I admit defeat in the eyes of the world, and that I feel myself guilty. Furthermore, it would set a precedent which would make American appearances impossible not only for myself but also other artists in similar situations; and these blackmailers—for this is what we are talking about, the blackmail maneuvers of a group—would be greatly encouraged to continue their actions. For a musical institution of your rank, I think you have shown no independence whatever.

Obviously, I cannot have the intention of conducting in a city where people will not do justice to my case. But before I can reach a negative decision, everything possible must be tried to inform the general public. I am ready to submit to the judgment of public opinion, but first the public must have the opportunity to make up its own mind."

Furtwängler then proposed several measures. He enclosed detailed information on his wartime activities, requesting that the Board publish it and await public reaction; he asked Ryerson to send this information to the conductors who had refused to appear with him, asking for a reconsidered statement and reminding them of the difficulty they had caused the Orchestra in spite of their long associations with it; if these conductors remained adamant after studying the material, he suggested they could be replaced by equally "outstanding" conductors such as Karajan, Kubelik and van Beinum. To carry out these measures, Furtwängler asked the Board to move slowly and carefully until the public rendered its judgment.

> "You see that I am still assuming my engagement will be possible. But if this is not possible, what compensation could you ever offer me for the enormous moral damage, not at all to be calculated in figures, that I am suffering in this case? Should you postpone the engagement for a year, thus avoiding current embarrassment now but still protecting our positions? I feel that surely you who bear the responsibility for my engagement, must now also be willing to defend your own conduct and myself. . . ."

As a postscript to his letter, Furtwängler added:

> "I have just spoken by telephone to Robert Murphy, United States Political Adviser for Germany; I explained the situation to him and he advised me *to hold my ground at all costs* in this engagement, in my own interest and the public interest, and above all not to make any premature decisions. If you need any further information about my Denazification or my role in Germany from Berlin, I request that you contact him."

The public furor in Chicago increased its intensity. The columns of letters-to-the-editor began to carry more messages defending Furtwängler than in the beginning, press comment was generally favorable, and statements on behalf of Furtwängler were made by Louis P. Lochner, longtime Chief of The Associated Press in Berlin before and early in the war; Friedelinde Wagner; Heinz Unger, a German-Jewish conductor resident in Toronto; and Hugo Kolberg, émigré former Concertmaster of the Berlin Philharmonic. Sigrid Schultz, who had earlier been correspondent in Berlin for the

Chicago Tribune, published an article marred by some errors
—that Furtwängler irritated the Nazis by his unenthusiastic
"German salutes," when in fact he had never given one; that
he had "received an elegant limousine as a surprise present"
on his birthday, that "his neighbors said he rather liked it,"
when in fact no such gift was ever made—but in its grudging
way, it offered some new information to readers in Chicago:

"Although Germany teemed with stories about artists kowtowing to Hitler and denouncing non-Nazis
and foreigners to the Gestapo and propaganda ministry,
I never heard such a report about Furtwängler that was
supported by enough evidence to make it seem reliable.
However, there was no doubt that whenever and wherever Furtwängler went on tour in foreign countries,
Nazis exploited them for propaganda purposes and Nazi
agents went with them to spy and agitate. Some of his
own musicians talked about their colleagues who had
gone out of their way to work for Nazis while abroad,
but I never heard such a charge against Furtwängler
himself.

'Furtwängler did not even indulge in the line of so
many other Germans who would tell foreigners they
met that nazism was not as bleak as pictured by the
foreign press,' Alexander Kipnis, famous basso, told me
when we compared notes on Furtwängler. 'Not for a
moment while I worked with Furtwängler in Germany,
France, or England did I believe that he favored the
Nazi régime. Only once did we discuss problems connected with it. Furtwängler told me that then he could
not believe the Nazi régime would last forever. Therefore, he said he wanted to try to keep or invite Jewish
artists, so that art could serve as Germany's bridge to
the world after the Nazi rule ended.'

While I was in Germany, Furtwängler had a well-
known German doctor, Johannes Ludwig Schmidt, who
was a glowing anti-Nazi and whom, to my personal
knowledge, the Gestapo tried twice to kill in fake accidents in 1939 and 1940. Later Schmidt was arrested

and thrown into a concentration camp. When Furtwängler became ill, he complained to authorities that he would not be able to conduct unless his doctor could treat him. Schmidt then was released for a few hours to treat Furtwängler.

To Americans who do not know terror, a conductor who asked for treatment from a physician under Nazi arrest might not seem brave, but in Germany people hastened to forget victims of Nazis because it was dangerous to know anyone in a concentration camp.

When we entered Berlin in 1945, I asked a friend about Furtwängler's war-time behavior. He told me that although Furtwängler held title in the state council he tried to sidestep some Nazi favors. There was a day in 1943 when, shortly before Furtwängler's birthday, Joseph Goebbels told the conductor that Hitler had chosen a wonderful present for him—a new villa. When Furtwängler told a friend about this, the friend warned him that the villa would work against him after the Nazis' defeat. Furtwängler said, 'But what can I do?' The friend advised him to go to Goebbels and tell him that he felt honored by the Führer's thoughtfulness but that his own house was unharmed by bombs, and that he would be grateful to the Führer if he assigned the villa to Germans who had lost their homes in bombings.

Furtwängler did just that but told friends that Goebbels had been very suspicious and displeased . . ."

This article, in spite of its errors and grudging tone, probably helped Furtwängler to some extent. It might be noted in passing that Dr. Schmidt was not released "for a few hours" to treat Furtwängler, but that he was allowed to do so once each week. He managed to survive the war solely because of this connection with Furtwängler.

Claudia Cassidy printed in the *Tribune* a letter commenting on the Chicago affair from a friend, Emerson Kailey, a local conductor living in Paris. He described the opening of the Paris musical season with Furtwängler leading the Vienna

112

Philharmonic, a concert which "received a delirious ovation rarely given in Paris." He added:

> "These concerts were sponsored by the French government in the state-owned opera house and broadcast over the state radio. Not one voice was raised in protest over Furtwängler, who has been a frequent guest conductor here since the war. The press was unanimous in acclaiming him and even the stagehands were enthusiastic. It must be remembered that the stagehands kept Lifar off the opera stage for a long time because of his purported Nazi sympathies during the war. They could have done the same to the famous German conductor if they had had the slightest reason. All of which makes it impossible to understand how 'super-patriots' in Chicago can find enough support to prevent his appearance with the Chicago Symphony. Do they think that he might contaminate the orchestra and the public by playing Beethoven as it should be?"

But, however more favorable press comment and readers' letters-to-the-editor were becoming, Furtwängler's opponents kept up their attack, and it was by these that the Chicago Board chose to be influenced. On January 10, Ryerson telegraphed:

> "Musical opposition very strong. Crowd with handbills and banners before Orchestra Hall at Thursday and Saturday concerts last week. Feel we must proceed with next season's arrangements on basis of a mutually satisfactory agreement for your withdrawal. Have made no statement to press and will not do so until receipt of further word from you but must immediately complete final arrangements for entire season and release to press not later than January fifteen."

Furtwängler realized now that he must take his defense into his own hands. On the next day he issued a statement

113

from Montreux that he had received numerous encouraging letters from America which indicated to him that "the American public on the whole does not approve methods like this boycott." He added:

"Among the musicians who want to keep me from America, I find, to my surprise, colleagues. When artists were being persecuted under the Hitler régime, it was I who did my best to keep them in the cause of the international solidarity of all artists, and today, four years after the end of the war, it is precisely artists who are persecuting me—although I must emphasize that none of those I defended, including Bruno Walter, Otto Klemperer, Max Reinhardt and Paul Hindemith, has ever said a word against me. But there are some artists who refuse to collaborate with me today only because I fought Hitler in his own country instead of fighting him from abroad."

In the same interview he mentioned the names of several Jewish musicians whose lives he had saved in the Hitler years, among whom were Carl Flesch, Professor Guido Adler, Viennese musicologist, Professor Robert Hernreid, then of Detroit, and several members of the Berlin and Vienna Philharmonic orchestras. He added that the Jewish organizations in Chicago were "wrongly informed."

These statements provoked energetic response from Rabbi Morton Berman, President of the Chicago division, American Jewish Congress, on January 14.

"If you knew nothing more of Furtwängler's relationship to nazism, his statement from Montreux would reveal that he has been well trained in Nazi propaganda techniques. Seeking to discredit the general protest against his appointment as conductor of the Chicago Symphony Orchestra, Furtwängler attributes the protest principally to Jewish organizations, while claiming that the American public itself disapproves of such a protest. This is the Nazi method.

Furtwängler preferred to swear fealty to Hitler. He accepted at Hitler's hands his reappointment as Director of the Berlin Philharmonic Orchestra. He was unfailing in his service to Goebbels' ministry of culture and propaganda.

With reference to Furtwängler's claim that he had helped individual Jews, it was my experience in Germany last summer, in listening to those who were being tried in Nuernberg, that every Nazi seeks to make the same claim. The token saving of a few Jewish lives does not excuse Mr. Furtwängler from official, active participation in a régime which murdered six million Jews and millions of non-Jews. Furtwängler is a symbol of all those hateful things for the defeat of which the youth of our city and nation paid an ineffable price."

A statement attributed to Fritz Busch appeared in the press, to the effect that Furtwängler lacked "the moral qualifications to conduct Beethoven." On January 17, the Berlin Philharmonic Orchestra wired the Chicago Board:

"We are astonished about the negative attitude against Dr. Furtwängler's appearance in Chicago. The Berlin Philharmonic Orchestra may from its own experience judge more strictly than people outside the activities of Dr. Furtwängler in the long years of our coöperation. We know well how much many colleagues of our Orchestra and other German artists were indebted to Dr. Furtwängler in the years from 1933 to 1945."

Two days later, James Petrillo, head of the American Federation of Musicians, stated that his union would probably refuse Furtwängler a work permit.

"Our contract contains a clause providing that any foreign artists brought in to play with or conduct the orchestra must be approved by the union local. We'll

115

reserve our decision, however, until the Chicago Orchestral Association decides whether or not Furtwängler is hired."

A spokesman for Local 10 of the musicians' union added:

"Furtwängler will never come to Chicago. He wouldn't have an orchestra to lead."

Menuhin appealed to Petrillo from Rome to grant the work permit. But this could not help. Furtwängler, realizing that further defense on his part was useless, wired the Board on January 19 the statement it had repeatedly requested in the past weeks:

"The protest of American artists against my coming to Chicago is based on news which the official propaganda in Nazi Germany chose to publish about me and not on truth. It is inconceivable that artists should perpetuate hatred indefinitely while all the world is longing for peace. In order to spare the Chicago Symphony Orchestra further difficulties I withdraw herewith from the already concluded contract."

On January 23, after the Board had released this statement, Claudia Cassidy noted in the *Tribune*:

"Wilhelm Furtwängler is not coming to Chicago—even the Orchestral Association finally got around to admitting what had been an open secret for weeks—but the controversy still rages . . ."[2]

---

[2] In this article Miss Cassidy quoted a photostatic copy of a letter from music critic David Hall to a third party, sent to her early in the controversy with his approval, which read in part: "As to the desirability of Furtwängler for the Chicago Symphony Orchestra, that is a matter that goes considerably beyond his past social record. I have heard the records that Furtwängler has made with the Vienna Philharmonic since the war, and they are, without exception, disappointing. The Brahms First Symphony, the Mozart Serenade in B-flat, and the Beethoven Coriolan Overture as recorded by him for H. M. V. were distressingly heavy-handed and woefully lacking in rhythmic

The battle over the appointment itself, however, had ended. Whatever assistance had been given to Furtwängler had not come from the Orchestral Association. In spite of his frequent warnings, the Board was genuinely shocked by the well-organized campaign of resistance, and had made no advance plans to counteract it. Already weakened by the unpopular dismissal of Rodzinski, enervated by the long and complicated negotiations to obtain Furtwängler's services, from the beginning of the controversy it was paralyzed. It made no disclosures of the intrigues in musical circles or of the pressures of boycott applied to American artists to whip them into line; it did not publish a telegram from Fritz Busch on January 14 emphatically denying the anti-Furt-wängler statement attributed to him in the press—this was published on November 20, 1949, eleven months later. It did not make public a letter from Felix Lederer, who explained how Furtwängler had saved his life and expressly requested its widest possible circulation; it did not publish the material Furtwängler had sent; it did not carry out any of his proposals. It had decided upon retreat, in fact, late in December, when the first serious protests began and the issue became national. Thereafter, all Furtwängler's pleas were in vain. During the controversy, communications with Furt-wängler had been difficult, as he fulfilled engagements in various European cities. There was a notable lack of coördi-nation between him and the Board, each side being confused and embarrassed by the other. But once the Board had de-cided not to fight back, it surrendered with dignity. The information which Furtwängler had sent in the hope that

strength and vitality. These weaknesses began to reveal themselves in small measure back in the late 1930s, but now they have apparently come to domi-nate his readings . . . In short, I hope to goodness Furtwängler does not come to Chicago—this for musical, not political reasons."

it would be used to help him win the struggle appeared in a statement published by Ryerson admitting defeat.

"To Guarantors, Sustaining Members,
and Season Ticket Subscribers.

Announcement of the fact that Dr. Furtwängler will not appear with us as guest conductor for the season 1949-1950 was released to the press by Dr. Furtwängler and by us on January 19th.

Because of your interest in this matter and in order that you may have an exact record of our position, we give you, herewith, a complete statement of the facts. Dr. Furtwängler cabled us on January 19th as follows:

'Edward L. Ryerson, President
Orchestral Association, Chicago

The protest of American artists against my coming to Chicago is based on the news which the official propaganda in Nazi Germany chose to publish about me and not on truth. It is inconceivable that artists should perpetuate hatred indefinitely while all the world is longing for peace. In order to spare Chicago Symphony Orchestra further difficulties I withdraw herewith from the already concluded contract.

Wilhelm Furtwängler'

Negotiations to bring Dr. Furtwängler to Chicago were commenced in the latter part of the summer of 1948. Before opening these negotiations the Board of Trustees of the Association carefully investigated his record and learned that the combined military authorities of the United States, Great Britain, France, and Russia, prior to July 1, 1947, gave a decision clearing Dr. Furtwängler of all Nazi affiliations. This decision is stated in the following letter:

118

'Office of Military Government for Germany (U.S.)
Office of the Director of Information Control APO 742

Berlin, Germany
1 July, 1947

Dr. Wilhelm Furtwängler
c/o Berlin Philharmonic, Berlin

Reference is made to your letter dated 28 June 1947.

The decision of the proper denazification authorities of the Berlin Kommandatura has cleared you completely of all nazi affiliations.

This office has, therefore, no objection concerning your cultural activities in the U. S. Zone of Germany. As the decision of the Kommandatura was made on a quadripartite level by all the four powers it is understood that you have been cleared also for cultural activities in all the four zones of Germany.

The fact that the denazification procedure lasted for more than one and a half years should prove that all efforts were made to investigate your case thoroughly. The final clearance should, therefore, be a great satisfaction for you.

Sincerely,
(signed)

Benno D. Frank
Chief, Theatre & Music Control'

After this clearance, Dr. Furtwängler appeared as guest conductor in England, at the Edinburgh Festival, in Scandinavia, in South America, and in Paris with the Paris Conservatory Orchestra. He took the Berlin Philharmonic Orchestra on a tour of England and in the initial concert of this tour Dame Myra Hess was the soloist. Everywhere his appearances were received with great acclaim.

The Board of Trustees was advised by Dr. Furt-wängler that because of his commitments in Europe and his desire to spend a substantial portion of his time in composition, he could not come to America for an extended period. However, a mutually satisfactory arrangement was reached for him to appear in Chicago as guest conductor for eight weeks of the coming season.

Unauthorized reports of our negotiations with Dr. Furtwängler appeared in the press both in this country and abroad; and as a result of this, protests were received by the Association from individuals as well as organizations objecting to his appearance in Chicago and attacking his record.

In December, after arrangements with Dr. Furt-wängler had been made, the Association proceeded to the matter of engaging other guest conductors for the rest of the season, and much to our surprise we were advised that some of the conductors felt they were unable to enter into a contract with the orchestra should Furt-wängler be engaged as one of its guests. Simultaneously a group of leading soloists made statements in the public press to the effect that they would not appear with the orchestra if Dr. Furtwängler appeared in Chicago. Other leading figures in the musical world made public objections to his appearance in America. Among these were Arturo Toscanini, Lily Pons, Vladimir Horowitz, Artur Rubinstein, Isaac Stern, and Gregor Piatigorsky.

We found clear evidence of a well organized opposition, not only from certain groups of the public but also in musical circles, seeking to boycott the orchestra in the event Dr. Furtwängler came to Chicago, and the Board became convinced that it would be unfair to ask such a distinguished musician to appear under adverse circumstances which might produce disorder and which would be greatly to the detriment of the high standard of performance which his conducting the orchestra should produce; nor did we wish to involve him personally in the unpleasantness which would result from this public opposition or to make our musical season in Chicago a focus for political controversy.

Dr. Furtwängler's withdrawal is after a full and friendly discussion with the officers of the Association. We are convinced that his record both politically and musically justified completely our plans for his engagement and that if he were permitted to appear under proper conditions the orchestra under his direction would have an opportunity of presenting the best in symphonic music that can be obtained anywhere in the world. As I stated above, Dr. Furtwängler was absolutely rehabilitated by the decision of the Commission of the Kommandatura in the middle of 1947.

For ten years before Hitler, Dr. Furtwängler was the outstanding figure in German musical life, occupying the most important posts in German and Austrian musical circles, directing the Berlin Philharmonic, the Berlin State Opera, the Vienna Philharmonic, the Vienna State Opera and at the Salzburg Festival. It is admitted even by many of his detractors that he was not a true Nazi. It is a well established fact that he retained his Jewish secretary against all opposition and used his influence to protect numerous individuals who were persecuted for racial reasons. He assisted some musicians with whom he was closely associated to leave Germany during the war. Furtwängler has declared that his appointment by Goering to the State Council was neither sought nor accepted by him, but he was advised that since it was an honorary title and not an office, only the government could remove him from this position.

In 1934 there was an open conflict between him and the Nazis regarding his defense of Paul Hindemith. He tried to resign as State Councilor and from all other positions, including that of Director of the State Opera, held by him in protest at this time, and never took up these positions again although he was later reoffered the Berlin and the Vienna Operas. He did not leave Germany because he believed that he could be of better use to his art and to many who were dependent upon him if he remained in that country. Subsequently he was only from time to time a guest at various institutes.

He was constantly in conflict with the authorities.

121

Rudolf Pechel, editor of the German Rundschau, one of the leaders of the German resistance movement, declared that Furtwängler was the only German musician considered as one of them. He refused to appear during the war in the occupied countries, Holland, Belgium, Norway and France. The tension between him and the German Government became acute in the year 1944 and he was warned by Hitler that any further intervention on his part in support of a non-Aryan would be considered an act of treason. In early 1945 he escaped arrest by the Gestapo by fleeing to Switzerland.

I would like to add a word of personal comment as to my position in connection with the Furtwängler negotiations. I knew that this decision would create some opposition and controversy. I was confident, however, in my belief that all of us who have made great sacrifices to bring the war to a victorious conclusion had done so in the hope that our victory would above all else bring about a world attitude of tolerance. Such a result should provide an opportunity for all individuals to develop and make use of their own talents and personalities in a world of people who have been freed from persecution and arrogance. To find that this attitude of tolerance has not yet been realized and accepted by many people, including even some outstanding artists, is tragic evidence of the fact that our victory as yet has not been complete.

Personally I have faith that in the near future these conflicts which are now emphasized by existing conditions of world unrest will be removed and that great artists and scientists of whatever nationality and lineage will be given an opportunity to fulfill their ambitions while at the same time giving us inspiration and enjoyment.

On behalf of the Board of Trustees,

Edward L. Ryerson
President

On February 4, Ryerson wrote Furtwängler a summation of events following his withdrawal:

"Since my last cable to you dated January 20, I have been assembling such material as has been released by the press and other items which might be of interest to you in connection with the public announcement that was made on the 19th of January. At the outset I want to express to you my very great appreciation for the fair-minded attitude that you have taken through all our recent difficulties and the outstanding spirit of co-operation which has been expressed in all your communications. I realize fully how disappointed you are with the way things have developed and you can rest assured that your disappointment is shared equally with us. We had looked forward with great anticipation to your appearance in Chicago as guest conductor to open our season in the Fall of 1949. Personally I had hoped that the contemplated engagement would lead to a continuance for longer periods of time. As you know, we originally approached the matter on the basis of your coming for the major part of one season and accepting the post of Musical Director but accepted your counter-suggestion that we proceed on the basis of your coming as guest conductor, because of the demands upon you for other commitments that you felt you could not neglect.

It is evident from the press comment and from numerous communications that I have had that a very strong reaction has been aroused in opposition to those who objected to your appearance in Chicago. I am satisfied that this reaction will continue to grow and that more and more people who are honest in their opinions will come to realize that you have been unjustly attacked and that the future of music in this country will be seriously damaged because of those who have taken it upon themselves to develop the opposition to your appearances in America.

I am enclosing a number of press clippings that will give you some idea as to how the announcement was covered by our local press in news items and some excellent editorial comment in support of your position and ours. Also I am enclosing a copy of a printed statement issued to our subscribers and supporters and which has been mailed to approximately five thousand individuals. We have received many letters and other messages of favorable comment as the result of this statement. Because of all this, I think you should feel reasonably well satisfied that the final handling of the matter was done in a way to redound very greatly to your credit and has improved your general public relationship rather than having injured it."

Furtwängler's secretary later wrote Kuyper that

"The cuttings which we received here were of great interest but we have the feeling that it is more or less a choice of favorable ones. Have no negative letters been published?"

and he replied,

"The clippings we sent you were fairly complete—we did not attempt any 'censorship.' The press was, on the whole, completely favorable."

Thus Furtwängler's contention that the general public was not against him, far from being a "Nazi propaganda technique" as Rabbi Berman had charged, was correct. Furtwängler's second contention that Jewish groups were "wrongly informed" about his case is best vindicated by a study of Rabbi Berman's statement itself.

It was a bitter satisfaction, however, that Furtwängler felt in hearing from Ryerson that he had in effect been correct all along in his analysis of the Chicago situation. This analysis is all the more striking because so little information was filtered to Furtwängler in the preceding weeks. After it was all over, he began to learn other details which further justified his views. His former colleague Fritz Zweig wrote from Los Angeles on March 6 that Bruno Walter had refused to support the anti-Furtwängler movement "in spite of being telephoned from all sides, particularly his colleagues" and had categorically denied the charge that Furtwängler had willingly coöperated with the Nazi régime. Furtwängler knew even more by the time he wrote Gilbert Back, his émigré Berlin Philharmonic violinist in Santa Monica, on April 14:

> "I spoke with Ansermet, who was recently here, and learned that the real spiritus rector of the movement against me was Ira Hirschmann. He succeeded in joining forces with Toscanini, and then a council of war was held in Toscanini's home. Some of the music agents were there as well . . ."

Andrew Schulhof, Ansermet's manager, was a friend of Hirschmann's and knew directly what had happened. One recalls Howard Taubman's article of January 6 in the *New York Times*, with its moralizing and evasive phrases: could this friend and soon to be biographer of Toscanini have missed this council of war before writing it? Could he have been unaware of the frantic telephoning, and pressures of boycott being applied to American musicians at that moment?

In the summer of 1949, at the Salzburg Festival, Furtwängler learned further details of the Chicago affair from American friends. Some months later he wrote Gilbert Back that he still could not understand the protest by Piatigorsky, a man who owed his discovery and early career to him alone:

> "It is possible, of course, that the same thing happened to Piatigorsky as to Milstein, who himself explained this to me here, and also apparently to Busch— namely that without their permission, protests against me were made up and published by certain interested parties."

Back replied on December 14, 1950, that he had recently seen Piatigorsky and that Piatigorsky denied ever having taken part in any action against Furtwängler. Could this third device—planting false protests in the press—have been unknown to Taubman when he wrote his article?

An epilogue to the Chicago affair was the article Claudia Cassidy published in the *Tribune* on September 4, 1949, based on an interview held in Salzburg that summer, and placing Furtwängler's role in Nazi Germany in its correct light. The Orchestral Association, encouraged by the popular support evident in the later stages of the controversy, had planned to invite Furtwängler in the following seasons as Guest Conductor; but once Rafael Kubelik had been engaged as Musical Director, it preferred not to subject him to comparison with an older colleague. Furtwängler understood this view, and wished Kubelik well.

VI

THERE WERE other, less public incidents. On October 18, 1951, Rudolf Bing, then the new Director of the Metropolitan Opera in New York, wrote Furtwängler to sound him out on opening the 1952 season with a new production of *Lohengrin*, to be staged by Herbert Graf, and presenting a second work as well, a revival of *Tristan und Isolde* or *Die Meistersinger*. Furtwängler was interested in the proposal, but there were difficulties in arranging his schedule to give him three months in New York. On November 8, Bing requested that he send a definite reply so that casting and scheduling details could be completed soon. He added:

> "With regard to the political implications of an invitation to you, I have not yet been able to obtain any sort of final information but my Board, in principle, welcomes the idea of my inviting you. We are still making one or two inquiries of important personalities and leaders of public opinion after which I will know definitely whether or not an official invitation on behalf of the Metropolitan Opera can be extended to you. However, I am still very hopeful that that will be the case . . ."

A week later he wrote

"It would be terribly unfair to you and us if we undertook too great a risk. Really serious objections could do the greatest damage to both of us and could make your appearance here impossible for a long time, after what happened in Chicago. The information reports we have gathered from really important persons in public life—four or five are in the highest government and press circles—were all unanimous, that it would be a most unfavorable time for your coming right now; however, they were of the opinion that things would be quite different a year from now . . . I am deeply disappointed, but as a foreigner I am myself too new here to challenge such advice. I will try again next year and hope that you personally are not angry with me—these problems are beyond my control and exceed my power."

In late 1952, Sol Hurok, in coöperation with the National Concert and Artists Corporation, was carrying on negotiations to bring the Vienna Philharmonic Orchestra to America. He had objected to Furtwängler's leading the tour, though Furtwängler was Principal Conductor of the Orchestra, and had gone ahead making advance bookings without mentioning the conductor's name. The Philharmonic stubbornly maintained that it was interested in a tour only if Furtwängler was its leader. On March 23, 1953, Hurok wrote the Executive Committee of the Philharmonic that he had received its recent cable to this effect and had given the whole matter further study. While he understood the Orchestra's loyalty to Furtwängler and while he respected Furtwängler's standing and accomplishments, Hurok said that he had to repeat that in his own judgment it would be exceedingly unwise and altogether impractical to attempt to carry out the complicated tour of the Orchestra under Furtwängler's direction. This was, he added, a situation for which he was not responsible and could not control, but it was for

128

this reason that he had steadfastly insisted on exercising his contractual rights to approve the choice of conductors for the tour. He assured the Committee that he was giving it the benefit of his best judgment and that he was speaking in its interest as well as his own when he said that Furtwängler would arouse a storm of controversy and protest that would jeopardize the success of the tour. His position, he went on, was made extremely difficult by the Committee's inability to carry out the terms of the agreement by accepting a conductor approved by him as musical director for the tour. His firm had gone to great expense in booking and promoting the engagements already scheduled for the Orchestra and would be placed in an embarrassing position with his clients if the Orchestra did not fulfill such commitments. It would certainly be necessary for the firm to look to the Orchestra for some restitution for expenses and damages in the event that it was finally unable to fulfill its part of the agreement. Hurok concluded by asking that the Executive Committee reconsider its position most carefully in order to see if there was not some way for it to replace Furtwängler and invite a conductor acceptable to him, in the best interests of the Orchestra and himself.

Furtwängler was then on tour, visiting Dortmund, Düsseldorf, Hanover, Baden-Baden, London, Paris, and Zürich, and communications were slow and difficult. But in a letter from the Executive Committee dated April 21, he learned that the Information Department of the Austrian General Consulate in New York had reported that

". . . Hurok had steadfastly refused to arrange an engagement with Dr. Furtwängler because Toscanini was determined to prevent Furtwängler's appearance in America at all costs."

On April 27, from Hanover, Furtwängler notified the Committee that it could either choose another leader or break with Hurok. He added that Hurok had no right to demand restitution, because in the earliest negotiations with Professor Rudolf Hanzl, on behalf of the Philharmonic, nothing had been mentioned about Hurok's right to decide the conductor or reject the Philharmonic's choice: in effect, the "contractual rights" whose violation he claimed as grounds for financial restitution did not exist. In a letter of May 5, he repeated the same point. The Philharmonic and circles in the Austrian government discussed a postponement of the tour for a year: but the Philharmonic Executive Committee of the Philharmonic insisted that Furtwängler be its leader on the American tour whenever it occurred. Hurok planned to come to Vienna to persuade it to accept his conditions. On June 22, Furtwängler wrote the Executive Committee a few days before Hurok's arrival:

"... By accident I have just learned from a reliable source that Hurok was one of the chief figures in the fight against my engagement in Chicago. When I think back, I am astonished that Professor Hanzl did not notice his attitude toward me, when he visited America."

This information came from Dr. Gerhardt von Westerman, Manager of the Berlin Philharmonic, in the course of correspondence concerning an American tour with the Berlin orchestra. Westerman wrote on June 19, 1953:

"Today I had a rather long conversation with Dr. Wolfgang Stresemann, who has lived in America as an exile for twenty years and seems to be very well informed on musical conditions there. He spoke indignantly about Hurok's behavior toward all Germans and particularly yourself. Hurok had written a letter to Bruno Walter in which he declared he would do everything in his power to prevent your Chicago engagement.

Bruno Walter gave Stresemann the letter to read and expressed his own indignation at Hurok's behavior, which caused Walter, in fact, to break relations with Hurok entirely."

The Berlin Philharmonic wanted a tour for the Spring of 1955; Furtwängler was undecided, in view of the priority of the Vienna orchestra and the still confused negotiations with Hurok. On June 24, the Viennese Committee wired that Hurok had been unable to come to Vienna but that telephone interviews had been arranged in advance with him. The Committee intended to present an ultimatum, a tour with Furtwängler or none at all.

The East German revolt decided the issue. The Bonn Government offered to underwrite passage expenses for the Berlin Philharmonic if Furtwängler would lead the tour to America. He wired the Vienna Philharmonic on July 6 that he would do so.

"In view of political situation and since realization of Berlin request dependent upon me alone, I consider this my duty as a German."

When he failed to dislodge the Vienna Philharmonic Committee from its position, Hurok retired from negotiations and the contract for the tour with Furtwängler in 1956 was released to the National Concert and Artists Corporation itself. Thus after an absence of twenty-six years, Furtwängler was to return to America with the Berlin and Vienna Philharmonic Orchestras. He died before he could bring either.

The obituaries were not much more accurate than his press had been in the past. The *New York Herald Tribune* reported on December 1, 1954:

"His personal distaste for controversy did not save him the furor which raged over his Nazi connections.

131

After the rise to power of National Socialism in Germany, he threw in his lot with the new régime. The Nazi purge of German music, designed to eliminate Jewish and radical elements, never received his open approval.

In 1934 his efforts to temper its severity forced his resignation from all official positions. But after a few months he was restored to favor and returned to his place on the podium of the Berlin Philharmonic Orchestra, and to his position as head of the German State Opera. Several times he conducted performances attended by Hitler.

. . . His only brush with the Nazis came in 1934 when he resigned from his official positions and made a public statement in defense of the music of the Swiss composer Paul Hindemith, who was accused of 'musical Bolshevism.' In 1935, after an interview with Hitler, he was back at his old posts . . ."

On the same day a dispatch from Bonn appeared in the *New York Times:*

". . . Dr. Furtwängler's towering reputation in the music world was overshadowed periodically by political considerations. His darkest hour was in 1948, when plans to have him conduct the Chicago Symphony Orchestra came to nought.

An outcry was raised that Dr. Furtwängler had been a Nazi sympathizer. Guest artists of international caliber notified Chicago that they would not appear on the same podium, subscribers grumbled, union leaders protested and the press across the country reflected the same viewpoint. Dr. Furtwängler, then in Europe, where he was accepted, bowed before the storm.

The merits of the case were difficult to assess because the facts appeared confused. Dr. Furtwängler had accepted high office from Hermann Goering and had been director of the Berlin Philharmonic Orchestra virtually throughout the Nazi régime, but he always argued that these things were done as a German and a musician and were without political significance.

When the Americans moved into Berlin after the war, the authorities adopted a stand four-square in opposition to Dr. Furtwängler. However on April 29, 1947, the Allied Kommandatura cleared him of the Nazi taint—several months after a German court had found the conductor not legally guilty though normally culpable.

Dr. Furtwängler satisfied his examiners with denials of misconduct, and no proof was forthcoming to convict him.

The most important fact brought out in his defense during Denazification proceedings was that he had saved the lives of several Jewish musicians and had protected Jewish members of the Berlin Philharmonic against National Socialist persecution. Mark Hindricks Leuschner, violinist, testified that Dr. Furtwängler had saved his life and that he had aided other Jewish musicians.

During the proceedings a letter was read, which Dr. Furtwängler had written to Goering. In the letter, the conductor stated that real artists should be protected no matter who they were. He also said in his letter, however, that he in some respects agreed with Goering 'about Jews' . . ."

The real background of the artists' protest to Chicago is, of course, not mentioned. The press across the country did not "reflect the same viewpoint." The Denazification Court had not found Furtwängler "not legally guilty though normally culpable." A letter to Goering was not read during the proceedings; this was the Open Letter to Goebbels, included above,[1] where Furtwängler attacks Jewish and non-Jewish dilettante artists for being destructive. Who made the facts of the case appear confused if not writers on the staff of the *Times?*

---

[1] Cf. pp. 34-5 above.

Still no mention was made of Furtwängler's escape from Gestapo arrest in 1945.

Errors continued to appear in the American press. Robert Charles Marsh, in an article entitled "Furtwängler and His Legacy" in *High Fidelity Magazine* of March 1955 wrote:

> ". . . Furtwängler realized after 1936 that, having chosen to remain in Germany, his position was dependent upon Nazi patronage, and the extent of that dependence is symbolically portrayed by his preparation of a gala birthday performance of *Die Meistersinger* for Hitler after the annexation of Austria in 1938. Resistance was over, and like millions of others, he did what his masters bade. Whatever the inner rebellion, the outer man conformed."

Hitler celebrated his birthday on April 20, 1938, in Berlin, by attending the premiere of Leni Riefenstahl's film on the 1936 Olympic Games, a performance attended by the diplomatic corps of the capital, including the American, British and French Ambassadors to Germany, and widely reported in the press at the time. On December 7, 1958, in a lengthy article on the New York Philharmonic-Symphony Orchestra, Howard Taubman wrote in the *Times*, referring to Toscanini's retirement in 1936:

> ". . . Though none could be expected to fill his shoes, someone would have to replace him. The likeliest candidate in eminence was Wilhelm Furtwängler, and he was mentioned in inner Philharmonic circles. But he had chosen to remain in Germany after Hitler came to power. There were too many people who could not stomach this association.
>
> Early in 1936 the Philharmonic announced its plans for the next season. The first ten weeks would be directed by Barbirolli, the last eight by Rodzinski and two weeks each in mid-season would be allotted to

the distinguished composer-conductors Igor Stravinsky, Georges Enesco, and Carlos Chavez."

The entire public controversy, and Toscanini's recommendation of Furtwängler for his post, were left unmentioned. David Ewen, in the 1959 edition of his *Encyclopedia of Concert Music* wrote:[2]

> "His intimate associations with the Nazi régime made Furtwängler persona non grata in the United States after the war, even though he was officially absolved of pro-Nazi activities in 1946. Several attempts to bring him back to the United States, first as conductor of the New York Philharmonic, then of the Chicago Symphony, collapsed in the face of public opposition."

Not all writers were inaccurate, however. Vincent Sheehan remarked on the postwar resistance movement against European musicians, and Furtwängler in particular:[3]

> ". . . But when it continued year after year one was forced to think that some relentless conspiratorial junta must be pulling the strings—some nonmusical purpose of importance was no doubt being served."

A more explicit analysis had already been given by Gilbert Back, in a letter to Furtwängler on April 19, 1949:

> ". . . A certain clique has taken advantage of the understandable Jewish hatred for the Nazis and to some extent for Germany itself, in order to use this for its own egotistical and wholly unpolitical purposes."

---

[2] *Encyclopedia of Concert Music* (New York, Hill and Wang, 1959), p. 168.
[3] *First and Last Love* (New York, Random House, 1956), pp. 256-7.

135

VII

MOST AMERICANS know Furtwängler only from recordings. There were several memorable performances available on the Brunswick label in the thirties, some of them later reissued by Deutsche Grammophon. But the most remarkable prewar records came from RCA Victor—the Beethoven *Fifth*, the Tchaikovsky *Pathétique*, the *Prelude and Liebestod* from Wagner's *Tristan und Isolde*, and the *Prelude and Good Friday Spell* from *Parsifal*, all with the Berlin Philharmonic. Three decades later, these remain the standard by which all other interpretations are judged. Fortunately, most of them are republished on long-playing records. In the postwar years very few recordings by Furtwängler were issued by Victor. On July 9, 1949, he wrote to Marks Levine of the National Concert and Artists Corporation:

> "I have a contract with His Master's Voice to which a contract with Victor is joined; yet Victor refused until now out of political reasons to take over any of the matrixes which I recorded with the Vienna Philharmonic Orchestra for H.M.V."

Four years later, on May 7, 1953, he wrote Gilbert Back in California:

"A year ago I renewed a long-term contract with His Master's Voice. H.M.V. had an agreement with Victor in America, that Victor take over the H.M.V. recordings and distribute them in America. From time to time I heard that my recordings were well received there. Yet again and again I have been warned that Victor is entirely in the hands of Toscanini and is thus especially interested in limiting the market of my records. Certain incidents in the recent past support this view."

In 1952 the appearance of His Master's Voice recordings in the United States meant that Americans in the larger cities, at least, had access to nearly all the performances Furtwängler had recorded in Vienna and London since 1947. Poorly distributed, rarely promoted, somewhat more expensive than domestic releases, their effect was necessarily limited.[1] A few titles appeared on other small labels. Victor eventually issued the complete *Tristan und Isolde* Furtwängler made with Kirsten Flagstad, and a posthumous Beethoven *Ninth*. There were many great recordings among those published, some of them never to be equalled. They were seldom recognized as such by our critics, for two reasons.

Some writers, especially those in New York, despised Furtwängler as a man because they believed him to have been a Nazi, as they loved Toscanini because they believed him to have been a political hero. This emotional involvement often disfigured their work. Thomas Mann, in his singularly sharp letter of July 1, 1947, while rejecting Furtwängler's proposal for a personal meeting, still paid tribute to him as the greatest conductor of our time; in his appearance on the CBS Television program *Small World* in March,

---

[1] David Hamilton has noted in his article, "Furtwängler vs. Toscanini, The Beethoven Symphonies," in *High Fidelity* (February, 1968) that . . . "Furtwängler's recordings received nothing like the publicity and circulation of Toscanini's; for RCA Victor, the latter represented a considerable investment of capital, while Furtwängler's were merely leased from EMI. Later, most were available here only as imports from Germany." (p. 66).

1960, Pablo Casals, who did not agree that Furtwängler should have remained in Nazi Germany, still paid homage to him as the greatest conductor he had known. But any such admission, at least while Toscanini was alive, was more than most American critics could make. There was, further, a vast gulf between the subjective Furtwängler approach to music and Toscanini's speedy precision, and some observers simply could not bridge it. Robert Charles Marsh perhaps best summarized their objections to Furtwängler's recordings.[2] But critical provincialism in itself was not so reprehensible. Occasionally suggestions were made that Furtwängler had deteriorated, that his performances were, in the words of one writer, "hardly what Furtwängler would have given in his best days." Certainly the older Furtwängler was different from the younger one. Every great artist develops constantly. But this development should not have been equated with deterioration because it pleased the critics less. Dimitri Mitropoulos felt otherwise about this, in a letter to Furtwängler dated August 21, 1953:

"Dearest Master:

I had no time to tell you goodbye, because I had to leave right away for New York, but I feel the necessity of thanking you once more for your kindness to me, and what a joy it was, after so many years, to find you greater than ever, with the maturity and serenity I have found in no other artist in my life . . .

I spoke about my enthusiasm to the Columbia Concerts, and found out, although it is still a secret, that your coming here is definite. I am sure you have nothing to worry about, and you will be celebrated as nobody else before . . ."

[2] *Toscanini and the Art of Orchestral Performance* (London, George Allen and Unwin, 1956), p. 78; cf. his *Toscanini and the Art of Conducting* (New York, Collier Books, 1962), p. 91.

The years after 1953 brought some changes. Toscanini was obliged to witness his orchestra ruthlessly disbanded by NBC as soon as he retired. Recordings made in Europe by Furtwängler, Klemperer, Kleiber, Casals, von Karajan, Fricsay, Krips, Jochum, Scherchen, Schuricht, Krauss, Knappertsbusch, Ansermet, van Beinum, Böhm, Kletzki, Kempe, Keilberth and others, introduced the American musical public to approaches quite different from the one it had been taught was "definitive." The great orchestras of Amsterdam, Berlin, London, Vienna, Israel and Leningrad enjoyed triumphant tours. Reflecting these changes, Paul Henry Lang commented in an article for the *New York Herald Tribune*, "The 'Definitive' Recording: Fraud, Fiction, and Myth," in 1959:

". . . every day we can observe the arrival of newly proclaimed 'final originals,' as well as the demise of those which only a few years ago were considered the unsurpassable norm. Toscanini is a good case in point. It used to be that only hysterical adjectives were acceptable when reviewing his recordings. Today it is no secret that while many of them remain supreme achievements, all of his Bach or Haydn, most of his Mozart, and a good deal of his Beethoven is not only questionable, but at times downright offensive."

In September 1962, Philip Hart published an unusually sensitive essay, "Furtwängler in Retrospect," in *The Musical Courier,* and there were several other thoughtful articles in musical journals in the following years. Reissues of Furtwängler recordings and new records made from concert performances were received more graciously here than during Futwängler's life. In his recent book, *The Great Conductors,*[3] Harold C. Schonberg of the *New York Times* devoted a chapter to Furtwängler which was more generous than Furt-

---

[3] *The Great Conductors* (New York, Simon and Schuster, 1967), pp. 270-80.

wängler admirers could expect from an American critic a decade ago.

The tragedy of Furtwängler's relations with America is not so much that he was denied recognition here; professional intrigues have always marked the musical world, quite apart from politics. It is the fact that a generation of our musicians grew up and matured deprived of his influence, of the opportunity to know him and perform with him, of sharing his artistic ideals, and of bringing to our musical tradition the enrichment that his presence could have given. But there are signs that this bleak picture is changing. Winthrop Sargent, in a Profile of Zubin Mehta in *The New Yorker* of December 16, 1967, noted:

> ". . . It is a curious thing that younger artists today should be reviving the Furtwängler style in opposition to the Toscanini style, but there is no doubt but this is what is happening. In Europe, and particularly in England, there is a whole school of younger artists who make collections of Furtwängler recordings, listen to them raptly, learn points of interpretation from them, and avidly discuss them. Hardly any of these artists are old enough to have heard Furtwängler perform, but they revere his style, and they strive to emulate it. Several of them are friends of Mehta's—among them the pianists Vladimir Ashkenazy, Daniel Barenboim, and Paul Badura-Skoda, the violinist Ivry Gitlis, and the cellist Jacqueline du Pré. These form a close-knit group. They admire each other, and though they are often on tour at opposite ends of the earth, they communicate almost daily by long-distance telephone. All of them take along portable phonographs on which to play Furtwängler records. Sometimes they even play passages to one another over the telephone and discuss them. 'That's where all our money goes,' Barenboim has said. Some of the recordings are standard issues, others are bootleg ones made in Russia from radio broadcasts during the Nazi régime and the war itself, and still others have been

presented to the members of the group by Furtwängler's widow. 'It's not a cult,' Mehta says. (Its members, though, are always referring to 'the Toscanini cult'). 'It's a clan. There is nothing unhealthy about it.'

Mehta does not believe, of course, in imitating any given Furtwängler interpretation; it is the general style he admires. Like most of the group, he never heard Furtwängler conduct; he once had a ticket to a performance in Vienna (it was to have been of Beethoven's Ninth Symphony), but before the concert could take place Furtwängler died. During his student days, Mehta came to know the members of the Vienna Philharmonic, which Furtwängler had frequently conducted, and he learned a great deal from them about the Furtwängler approach, which he has since attempted to transfer to both the Montreal Symphony and the Los Angeles Philharmonic."

One cannot accurately speak of "reviving" the Furtwängler style in Europe, because it has continued to be the ideal of conducting there since Furtwängler's death in 1954. But we should notice how much Furtwängler's records have gripped the imaginations of these gifted artists. Equally striking is the report by Martin Bernheimer in the *Times* of March 10, 1968, concerning another young musician, Andre Previn, conductor of the London Symphony and the Houston Symphony Orchestras:

"Returning to his birthplace in Germany represents 'a monstrous problem of conscience.' Previn's family left Berlin in 1939, not without personal, sociological and political scars. He has carried around some bitter memories for almost three decades. But, crucially, he has also retained at least one overwhelming recollection of Berlin: an all-Brahms concert with Furtwängler and the Philharmonic. His father, a music-loving judge and attorney, took Andre to hear it when the boy was only 5.

When the Berlin Philharmonic invited Previn to con-

141

duct, he accepted on one condition—that the program embrace the same works he heard played by Furtwängler and the orchestra at that concert 33 years ago. The condition was granted: Previn's debut as conductor in Berlin will have, as its vehicles, the 'Tragic' Overture, the Violin Concerto, and the Fourth Symphony."

Another remarkable incident occurred in May, 1969, when Irving Kolodin, one of our most cautious and perceptive critics, welcomed the arrival of a brilliant young conductor of whom he had not heard: Carlos Paita's recording of Wagner's *Prelude and Liebestod* from *Tristan und Isolde* was judged ". . . the best to be heard in years, on a plane of musical perfection and emotional eloquence rarely heard since the passing of Furtwängler, Knappertsbusch, Beecham, and the other great names of this literature (not excluding Toscanini) . . . Paita is described as a musician of mixed Hungarian and Italian stock, born in Argentina in 1932. His idol, I note, was Furtwängler, whom he heard at the Colon in the early Fifties . . ."

And in the February 1970 issue of *High Fidelity*, the American conductor Henry Lewis wrote of Furtwängler: "Here was a conductor who has been for me an object of admiration because of his originality, individuality, and honesty. He rightfully freed himself from slavish adherence to the printed note, realizing that the notes as engraved in a score are symbols—much like dance notation. The notation is not the essence of the music, not the spirit; Furtwängler had that rare and great ability to go beyond the printed score, to arrive at and to show us what the music is really about." Lewis had some sharp words on the musical criticism of his own formative years: "There was a time when I was discouraged about becoming a musician because concerts had become such funereal experiences. Thankfully we are emerging from the musicological stage of the Fifties, when a critic's highest praise was 'a no-nonsense performance.' This brief but damaging encounter with literalism has ended, and today's young conductors offer real hope for the future."

At the time of Furtwängler's death it was noted that he had stamped his seal on younger musicians who heard him. His achievement continues to influence another generation he never knew. Perhaps it is not too much to trust that these exponents of his style will show us the nature of inspired musicianship in a way that Furtwängler, after 1927, was not allowed to do.

INDEX

Abendroth, H., 38
Allied Kommandatura, 82, 88, 119, 121, 133
American Federation of Labor, 53
American Federation of Musicians, 53, 115
American Jewish Congress, 114
Ansermet, E., 67, 101-2, 106, 108, 125, 139
Ashkenazy, V., 140
Associated Press, Berlin, 31, 52, 110

Back, G., 69, 86, 125-6, 135, 136
Badura-Skoda, P., 140
Barbirolli, J., 134
Barenboim, D., 140
Bayreuth Festival, 55-6
Beecham, Sir T., 30, 58, 142
Berlin Philharmonic Orchestra, 10, 33, 47, 60, 65-6, 71, 85, 89, 94-5, 115, 121, 130-32, 136, 141-2
Berlin *Philharmonie*, 37, 49, 82
Berlin State Opera, 47, 51-3, 58, 66, 74, 121
Berman, Rabbi M., 114-5, 124
Bernheimer, M., 142
Bienenfeld, E., 40
Bing, R., 127-8
Bloch, S., 27
Böhm, K., 139
Borchard, L., 60
Boston Symphony Orchestra, 108
Brailowsky, A., 102
Bürckel, J., 57
Busch, A., 33, 91
Busch, F., 10, 104, 115, 117, 125

Carnegie Hall, 10, 12, 17, 18, 28
Casals, P., 10, 42, 138-9

Cassidy, C., 112, 116, 126
Celibidache, S., 60
Chavez, C., 135
Chicago Orchestral Association, *see* Chicago Symphony Orchestra, Board of Directors, 97-8, 106, 109-10, 113, 116-7, 120-21
Chicago Symphony Orchestra, 97ff., 113, 116, 132, 135
Chicago Tribune, 99, 111, 112, 116, 126
Clark, D., 69ff., 105
Columbia Broadcasting System (CBS Television), 137-8
Columbia Concerts Corporation, 46, 138
Cortot, A., 42-3

Damrosch, W., 18
Denazification Tribunal, 67ff., 87-8, 94, 119, 133
de Sabata, V., 72, 104
Deutsche Allgemeine Zeitung, 34, 45
Deutsche Grammophon, 136
Dobrowen, I., 89
Downes, O., 10-11, 13-16, 21ff.
du Pré, J., 140

Eisenhower, Gen. D. D., 60
Elliot, J., 89-90
Enesco, G., 135
Ewen, D., 135

Flagstad, K., 137
Flesch, C., 39, 114
Frank, B. D., 119
Funk, W., 33
Furtwängler, W., *passim*

146

147